COGNITION-BASED ASSESSMENT & TEACHING

of Multiplication and Division

Michael T. Battista

COGNITION-BASED ASSESSMENT & TEACHING
of Multiplication and Division

Building on
Students'
Reasoning

HEINEMANN
Portsmouth, NH

Heinemann

361 Hanover Street

Portsmouth, NH 03801–3912

www.heinemann.com

Offices and agents throughout the world

Library of Congress Cataloging-in-Publication Data

Battista, Michael T.

   Cognition-based assessment and teaching of multiplication and division : building on students' reasoning / Michael Battista.

       p. cm.

   Includes bibliographical references.

   ISBN-13: 978-0-325-04344-9

   ISBN-10: 0-325-04344-2

   1. Multiplication—Study and teaching (Elementary).   2. Division—Study and teaching (Elementary). 3. Reasoning—Study and teaching (Elementary).   4. Thought and thinking—Study and teaching (Elementary).   5. Cognitive learning.   I. Title.

QA115.B377 2012

372.7'2—dc23
                                            2011043543

Editor: Katherine Bryant

Production: Victoria Merecki

Typesetter: Publishers' Design & Production Services, Inc.

Interior and cover designs: Monica Crigler

Website developer: Nicole Russell

Manufacturing: Steve Bernier

Printed in the United States of America on acid-free paper

16   VP   4 5

Contents

$\times \div$

Acknowledgments

×÷

I would like to thank the numerous students, parents, teachers, school districts, and research assistants who participated in the CBA project.

I especially want to thank Kathy Battista who has provided invaluable advice and work throughout the CBA project.

Research and development of CBA was supported in part by the National Science Foundation under Grant Numbers 0099047, 0352898, 554470, and 838137. The opinions, findings, conclusions, and recommendations, however, are those of the author and do not necessarily reflect the views of the National Science Foundation.

—Michael Battista

Introduction

$\times \div$

Traditional mathematics instruction requires all students to learn a fixed curriculum at the same pace and in the same way. At any point in traditional curricula, instruction *assumes* that students have already mastered earlier content and, based on that assumption, specifies what and how students should learn next. The sequence of lessons is fixed; there is little flexibility to meet individual student's learning needs. Although this approach appears to work for the top 20 percent of students, it does not work for the other 80 percent (Battista, 1999, 2001). And even for the top 20 percent of students, the traditional approach is not maximally effective (Battista, 1999, 2001). For many students, traditional instruction is so distant from their needs that each day they make little or no learning progress and fall farther and farther behind curriculum demands. In contrast, Cognition-Based Assessment (CBA) offers a cognition-based framework to support teaching that enables *all* students to understand, make personal sense of, and become proficient with mathematics.

The CBA approach to teaching mathematics focuses on deep understanding and reasoning, within the context of continually assessing and understanding students' mathematical thinking then builds on that thinking instructionally. Rather than teaching predetermined, fixed content at times when it is inaccessible to many students, the CBA approach focuses on maximizing *individual student progress no matter where students are in their personal development*. As a result, you can move your students toward reasonable, grade-level learning benchmarks in maximally effective ways. Designed to work with any curriculum, CBA will enable you to better understand and respond to your students' learning needs and help you choose instructional activities that are best for your students.

There are six books in the CBA project:

- *Cognition-Based Assessment and Teaching of Place Value*
- *Cognition-Based Assessment and Teaching of Addition and Subtraction*
- *Cognition-Based Assessment and Teaching of Multiplication and Division*
- *Cognition-Based Assessment and Teaching of Fractions*
- *Cognition-Based Assessment and Teaching of Geometric Shapes*
- *Cognition-Based Assessment and Teaching of Geometric Measurement*

Any of these books can be used independently, though you may find it helpful to refer to several because the topics covered are interrelated.

Critical Components of CBA

The CBA approach emphasizes three key components that support students' mathematical sense making and proficiency:

- clear, coherent, and organized research-based descriptions of students' development of meaning for core ideas and reasoning processes in elementary school mathematics;
- assessment tasks that determine how each student is reasoning about these ideas; and
- detailed descriptions of the kinds of instructional activities that will help students at each level of reasoning about these ideas.

More specifically, CBA includes the following essential components.

Levels of Sophistication in Student Reasoning

For many mathematical topics, researchers have found that students' development of mathematical conceptualizations and reasoning can be characterized in terms of "levels of sophistication" (Battista, 2004; Battista and Clements, 1996; Battista et al., 1998; Cobb and Wheatley, 1988; Fuson et al., 1997; Steffe, 1988, 1992; van Hiele, 1986). Chapter 2 presents a framework that describes the development of students' thinking and learning about multiplication and division in terms of these levels. This framework describes the "cognitive terrain" in which students' learning trajectories occur, including:

- the levels of sophistication that students pass through in moving from their intuitive ideas and reasoning to a more formal understanding of mathematical concepts;
- cognitive obstacles that students face in learning; and
- fundamental mental processes that underlie concept development and reasoning.

Figure 1 sketches the cognitive terrain that students must ascend to attain understanding of multiplication and division of whole numbers. This terrain starts with students' preinstructional reasoning about multiplication and division, ends with a formal and deep understanding of multiplication and division, and indicates the cognitive plateaus reached by students along the way. Not pictured in the sketch are sublevels of understanding that may exist at each plateau level. Note that students may travel slightly different trajectories in ascending through this cognitive terrain, and they may end their trajectories at different places depending on the curricula and teaching they experience.

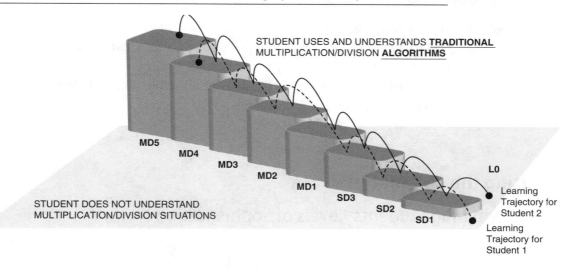

Figure 1. Levels of Sophistication Plateaus and Two Learning Trajectories for Multiplication and Division

A Note About the Student Work Samples

Chapter 2 includes many examples of students' work, which are invaluable for understanding and using the levels. All of these examples are important, for they show the rich diversity of student thinking at each level. However, the first time you work through the materials, you may want to read only a few examples for each type of reasoning—just enough examples to comprehend the basic idea of the level. Later, as you use the assessment tasks and instructional activities with your students, you can sharpen your understanding by examining additional examples both in the level descriptions and in the level examples for each assessment task.

Assessment Tasks

The Appendix contains a set of CBA assessment tasks that will enable you to determine your students' mathematical thinking and precisely locate students' positions in the cognitive terrain for learning that idea. These tasks not only assess exactly what students can do, they also reveal students' reasoning and underlying mathematical cognitions. The tasks are followed by a description of what each level of reasoning might look like for each assessment task. These descriptions will help you pinpoint your students' positions in the cognitive terrain of learning.

Using CBA assessment tasks to determine which levels of sophistication students are using will help you pinpoint students' learning progress, know where students should proceed next in constructing meaning and competence for the idea, and decide which instructional activities will best promote students' movement to higher levels of reasoning. It can also help guide your questions and responses in classroom discussions and in students' small-group work. The CBA website at www.heinemann .com/products/E04344.aspx includes additional assessment tasks that you can use to further investigate your students' understanding of multiplication and division.

Instructional Suggestions

Chapters 3 and 4 provide suggestions for instructional activities that can help students progress to higher levels of reasoning. These activities are designed to meet the needs of students at each CBA level. The instructional suggestions are not meant to be comprehensive treatments of topics. Instead, they are intended to help you understand what kinds of tasks may help students make progress from one level/ sublevel to the next higher level/sublevel.

Using the CBA Materials

Determining Students' Levels of Sophistication

There are several ways that you can use CBA assessment tasks to determine students' levels of sophistication in reasoning about multiplication and division.

Individual Interviews

The most accurate way to determine students' levels of sophistication is to administer the CBA assessment tasks in individual interviews with students.[1] For many students, interviews make describing their thinking much easier; they are perfectly capable of describing their thinking orally but have difficulty doing it in writing. Individual interviews also allow teachers to ask probing questions at just the right time, which can be extremely helpful in revealing students' thinking. (Beyond assessment purposes, the individual attention that students receive in individual assessment interviews can also provide students with added motivation, engagement, and learning.)

Whole-Class Discussion

In an "embedded assessment" model—in which assessment is embedded within instruction—you can give an assessment task to your whole class as an instructional activity. Each student should have a student sheet with the task on it. Students do all their work on their student sheets and describe in writing how they solve the task. When all the students are finished writing their descriptions of their solution methods, have a class discussion of those methods. For instance, many teachers have a number of individual students present their solutions on an overhead projector or a document-projection device. As students describe their thinking, ask questions that encourage students to provide the detail you need to determine what levels of reasoning they are using. Also, at times, you can revoice or summarize students' thinking in ways that model good explanations (but be sure that you provide accurate descriptions of what students say instead of formal versions of their reasoning). After

---

[1] For helpful advice on scheduling and conducting student interviews, see Larry Buschman. (December 2001). Using Student Interviews to Guide Classroom Instruction: An Action Research Project. *Teaching Children Mathematics*, pp. 222–227.

each different student explanation, you can ask how many students used the strategy described. It is important that you not only have students orally describe their solution strategies but that you talk about how they can write and represent their strategies on paper. For instance, after a student has orally described his strategy, ask the class, "How could you describe this strategy on paper so that I would understand it without being able to talk to you?"

Another way to see if students' written explanations accurately describe their solution strategies is to ask students to come up to your desk and tell you individually what they did, which you can then compare to what they wrote.

Individual and Small-Group Work

You can also determine the nature of students' reasoning by circulating around the room as students are working individually or in small groups on CBA assessment tasks or instructional activities. Observe student strategies and ask students to describe what they are doing as they are doing it. Seeing students actually work on problems often provides more accurate insights into what they are doing and thinking than merely hearing their explanations of their completed solutions (which sometimes do not match what they did). Also, as you talk to and observe students during individual or small-group problem solving, for students who are having difficulty accurately describing their work, write notes to yourself on students' papers that tell you what they said and did (these notes are descriptive, not evaluative).

The Importance of Questioning

Keep in mind that the more students describe their thinking, the better they will become at explaining that thinking, especially if you guide them toward providing increasingly accurate and detailed descriptions of their reasoning. For instance, if a student says, "I counted," ask, "How did you count? Count out loud to show me what you did. How could you write about what you did?"

As a more specific example, consider a student working on the problem, "Mary has 4 bags and 5 apples in each bag. How many apples does Mary have?" Suppose Jim writes "$4 \times 5 = 20$" as his explanation of his strategy. Ask additional questions.

Teacher: *What did you do to figure out that $5 \times 4 = 20$?*

Jim: *I counted.*

Teacher: *How did you count? Count out loud for me.*

Jim: *5, 10, 15, 20.*

Teacher: *Okay, that's a great way to solve the problem. How could you write that on your sheet?*

Jim: *I could write that I counted.*

Teacher: *Great. And what else could you write so I know how you counted?*

Jim: *I don't know.*

Teacher: *What numbers did you say when you counted?*

Jim: *5, 10, 15, 20.*

Teacher: *So, you could write these numbers on your sheet.*

Listed below are some questions that can be helpful in conducting individual interviews, interacting with students during small-group work, or conducting a classroom discussion of an assessment task.

- That's interesting; tell me what you did.
- Tell me how you found your answer.
- How did you figure out this problem?
- I'd really like to understand how you're thinking; can you tell me more about it?
- Why did you do that?
- What were you thinking when you moved these objects?
- Did you check your answer to see whether it is correct? How?
- Explain your drawing to me.
- What do these marks that you made mean?
- What were you thinking when you did this part of the problem?
- What do you mean when you say…?

Monitoring the Development of Students' Reasoning

The CBA materials are designed to help you assess levels of reasoning, not levels of students. Indeed, a student might use different levels of reasoning on different tasks. For instance, a student might operate at a higher level when using physical materials such as place-value blocks than when she does not have physical materials to support her thinking. Also, a student might operate at different levels on tasks that are familiar to her or that she has practiced as opposed to tasks that are totally new to her. So, rather than attempting to assign a single level to a student, you should analyze a student's reasoning on several assessment tasks then develop an overall profile of how she is reasoning about the topic. An example of how this is done appears in Chapter 2.

To carefully monitor and even report to parents the development of student reasoning about particular mathematical topics, many teachers keep detailed records of students' CBA reasoning levels during the school year. To do this, choose several CBA assessment tasks for each major mathematical topic you will cover during the year. Administer these tasks to all of your students either as individual interviews or as written work at several different times during the school year (say, before and after each curriculum unit dealing with the topic). In addition to noting the tasks used and the date, record what levels each student used on the tasks.

Differentiating Instruction to Meet Individual Students' Learning Needs

You can tailor instruction to meet individual students' learning needs in several ways.

Individualized Instruction

The most effective way to meet students' learning needs is to work with them individually using the levels and tasks to precisely assess and guide students' learning. This approach is an extremely powerful way to maximize an individual student's learning.

Instruction by CBA Groups

Another effective way of meeting students' needs is putting students into groups based on their CBA levels of reasoning about a mathematical topic. You can then look to the instructional suggestions for tasks that will be maximally effective for helping the students in each group. For instance, you might have three or four groups in your class, each consisting of students who are reasoning at about the same CBA levels and need the same type of instruction.

Whole-Class Instruction

Another approach that many teachers have used successfully is selecting sets of tasks that all students in a class can benefit from doing. You do this by first determining the different levels of reasoning among students in the class. Then, as you consider possible instructional tasks, ask yourself,

- "How will students at each level of reasoning attempt to do this task?"
- "Can students at different levels of reasoning *succeed* on the task by using different strategies?" (Avoid tasks that some students will not have any way of completing successfully.)
- "How will students at each level benefit by doing the task?"
- "Will seeing how different students do the task help other students progress to higher levels of thinking because they are ready to hear new ways of reasoning about the task?"

Also, sets of tasks can be sequenced so that initial problems target students using lower levels of reasoning while later tasks target students using higher levels.

Another way to individualize whole-class instruction is to ask different questions to students at different levels as you circulate among students working in small groups. For instance, for students who are operating on numbers as collections of ones, you might ask if there is another way to count to solve the problem—can they use skip-counting? On the same problem, for students who are already skip-counting, you might ask if they can do the problem without counting (say, by using number properties and derived facts). Knowledge of CBA levels is invaluable in devising good questions and in asking appropriate questions for different students. In fact, when preparing to teach a lesson, many teachers use levels-of-sophistication descriptions to think about the kinds of questions they will ask students who are functioning at different levels.

Choosing which students to put into small groups for whole-class inquiry-based instruction is also important. If you think of your students' CBA levels of reasoning on a particular type of task as being divided into three groups, you might put students in the high and middle groups together or students in the middle and low groups together. Generally, putting students in the high and low groups together is not effective because their thinking is likely to be too different.

Assessment and Accountability

As a consequence of state and federal testing and accountability initiatives, most school districts and teachers are looking for materials and methods that will help them achieve state performance benchmarks. CBA is a powerful tool that can help you help your students achieve these benchmarks by:

- monitoring students' development of reasoning about core mathematical ideas;
- identifying students who are having difficulties learning these ideas and diagnosing the nature of these difficulties;
- understanding the nature of weaknesses identified by annual state mathematics assessment results *along with causes for these weaknesses*; and
- understanding a framework for remediating student difficulties in conceptually and cognitively sound ways.

Moving Beyond Deficit Models

The CBA materials can help you move beyond the "deficit" model of traditional diagnosis and remediation. In the deficit model, teachers wait until students fail before attempting to diagnose and remediate their learning problems. CBA offers a more powerful, preventive model for helping students. By using CBA materials to appropriately pretest students on core ideas that are needed for upcoming instructional units, you can identify which students need help and the nature of the help they need before they fail. By then using appropriate instructional activities, you can help students acquire the core knowledge needed to be successful in the upcoming units—making that instruction effective rather than ineffective for these students.

The Research Base

Not only have these materials gone through extensive field testing with both students and teachers, but the CBA approach is also consistent with major scientific theories describing how students learn mathematics *with understanding*. These theories agree that mathematical ideas must be personally constructed by students as they intentionally try to make sense of situations. Furthermore, to be effective, mathematics teaching must carefully guide and support students' construction of personally meaningful mathematical ideas (Baroody and Ginsburg, 1990; Battista, 1999, 2001; Bransford, Brown, and Cocking, 1999; De Corte, Greer, and Verschaffel, 1996; Greeno, Collins, and Resnick, 1996; Hiebert and Carpenter, 1992; Lester, 1994; National Research Council, 1989; Prawat, 1999; Romberg, 1992; Schoenfeld, 1994; Steffe and Kieren, 1994; von Glasersfeld, 1995). Research shows that when students' current ideas and beliefs are ignored, their development of mathematical understanding suffers. And conversely, "There is a good deal of evidence that learning is enhanced when teachers pay attention to the knowledge and beliefs that learners bring to a learning task, use this knowledge as a starting point for new instruction, and monitor students' changing conceptions as instruction proceeds" (Bransford et al., 1999, p. 11).

The CBA approach is also consistent with research on mathematics teaching. For instance, based on their research in the Cognitively Guided Instruction program, Carpenter and Fennema concluded that teachers must "have an understanding of the general stages that students pass through in acquiring the concepts and procedures in the domain, the processes that are used to solve different problems at each stage, and the nature of the knowledge that underlies these processes" (1991, p. 11). Indeed, a number of studies have shown that when teachers learn about such research on students' mathematical thinking, they can use that knowledge in ways that positively impact their students' mathematics learning (Carpenter et al., 1998; Cobb et al., 1991; Fennema and Franke, 1992; Fennema et al., 1996; Steff and D'Ambrosio, 1995). These materials will enable you to:

- develop a detailed understanding of your students' current reasoning about specific mathematical topics and
- choose learning goals and instructional activities to help your students build on their current ways of reasoning.

Indeed, these materials provide the kind of coherent, detailed, and well-organized research-based knowledge about students' mathematical thinking that research has indicated is important for teaching (Fennema and Franke, 1992).

Research also shows that using formative assessment can produce significant learning gains in all students (Black and Wiliam, 1998). Furthermore, formative assessment can be especially helpful for struggling students, so it can reduce achievement gaps in mathematics learning. The CBA materials offer teachers a powerful type of *formative assessment* that monitors students' learning in ways that enable teaching to be adapted to meet students' learning needs. "For assessment to function formatively, the results have to be used to adjust teaching and learning" (Black and Wiliam, 1998, p. 142). To implement high-quality formative assessment, the major question that must be asked is, "Do I really know enough about the understanding of my pupils to be able to help each of them?" (Black and Wiliam, 1998, p. 143). CBA materials help answer this question.

Using CBA Materials for RTI

Response to Intervention (RTI) is a school-based, tiered prevention and intervention model for helping all students learn mathematics. Tier 1 focuses on high-quality classroom instruction for all students. Tier 2 focuses on supplemental, differentiated instruction to address particular needs of students within the classroom context. Tier 3 focuses on intensive individualized instruction for students who are not making adequate progress in Tiers 1 and 2.

CBA can be effectively used for all three RTI tiers. For Tier 1, CBA materials provide extensive, research-based descriptions of the development of students' learning of particular mathematical topics. Research shows that teachers who understand such information about student learning teach in ways that produce greater student achievement. For Tier 2, CBA descriptions enable you to better understand and monitor each student's mathematics learning through observation, embedded assessment, questioning, informal assessment during small-group work, and formal assessment. You can then choose instructional activities that meet your students' learning needs—whole-class tasks that benefit students at all levels; different tasks for small groups of students at the same levels; individualized supplementary student work. For Tier 3, CBA assessments and level-specific instructional suggestions provide road maps and directions for giving struggling students the long-term individualized instruction sequences they need.

Supporting Students' Development of Mathematical Reasoning

CBA materials are designed to help students move to higher levels of reasoning. It is important, however, that instruction not *demand* that students "move up" the levels with insufficient cognitive support. Such demands result in students rotely memorizing procedures that they cannot make personal sense of. *Jumps in levels are made internally by students, not by teachers or the curriculum.* This does not mean that students must progress through the levels with no help. Teaching helps students by providing them with the right kinds of encouragement, support, and challenges—having students work on problems that stretch, but do not overwhelm, their reasoning, asking good questions, having them discuss their ideas with other students, and sometimes showing them ideas that they don't invent themselves. But when we show students ideas, we should not demand that they use them. Instead, we should try to get students to adopt new ideas because students make personal sense of the ideas and see the new ideas as better than the ideas they currently have.

Chapter 1

Introduction to Understanding Multiplication and Division

×÷

There are two critical components in the development of students' reasoning about multiplication and division of whole numbers. First, students must understand what the operations mean and recognize when each is appropriate in problem solving. Second, students must understand and become proficient with strategies for performing computations for these operations.

What It Means to Multiply and Divide

In typical multiplication problems, we are given the number of equivalent groups and the number in each group and asked to find the total. In typical division problems, we are given the total, or product, and one of the factors (number of equivalent groups *or* the number in each group) and asked to find the other factor.

There are two major division situations. In *measurement* division, we are given the total number of objects and asked how many equivalent groups of a given size can be made from the total (for example, how many groups of 3 are in 15, or what is the *measure* of 15 if we take 3 as the *unit of measure*?). In *partitive* division, we are given the total number of objects and asked how many objects will be in each group if the objects are partitioned (divided, separated) into a given number of equivalent groups (for example, if 15 tennis balls are *partitioned* into 5 equal groups, how many will be in each group?).

The major meanings for multiplication and division are summarized in Figure 1.1. Note that although the examples describe situations that focus on sets of discrete objects (e.g., 5 tennis balls), the same situations can occur for continuous quantities (e.g., 5 inches), which can be more difficult for students to conceptualize.

Figure 1.1. Multiplication and Division Meanings

Multiplication: (*number of equivalent groups*) × (*number in each group*) = *total*

Example: Jon has 5 cans of tennis balls. Each can has 3 balls in it. How many tennis balls does Jon have altogether? [*5 × 3 = 15; 5 groups of 3 makes a total of 15*]

Measurement Division: (*number of objects*) ÷ (*number of objects in a group*) = (*number of equivalent groups*)

Example: Jon has 15 tennis balls. If he puts 3 tennis balls in each can, how many cans does he need? [*15 ÷ 3 = 5; if there are 15 total and 3 in each group then there are 5 groups*]

Partitive Division: (*number of objects*) ÷ (*number of equivalent groups*) = (*number of objects in a group*)

Example: Jon has 15 tennis balls. If he puts the same number of tennis balls in each of 5 cans, how many balls will be in each can? [*15 ÷ 5 = 3; if there are 15 total and 5 equal groups then there are 3 in each group*]

Relationship Between Measurement and Partitive Division

Many students are puzzled by the two different meanings for division. It is often helpful to these students to see how the measurement and partitive meanings are related for a specific problem. To see how the measurement meaning applies to the partitive division example in Figure 1.1, think of putting 1 ball into each of 5 cans 3 times (see Figure 1.2). The first time, we distribute 5 balls, 1 into each of 5 cans; we subtract 5 from 15 to see that there are 10 remaining balls. The second time, we distribute 5 balls, 1 into each of 5 cans, and subtract 5 from 10 balls to see that there are 5 remaining balls. The third time we distribute 5 balls, 1 into each of 5 cans, and then subtract 5 balls to see that we have none left. When we ask how many balls are in each can (partitive), we are also asking how many sets of 5 are in 15 or how many times we can subtract 5 from 15 (measurement). So for a set of 15 objects, the number of objects in a group if there are 5 equal groups equals the number of groups of 5 objects.

Figure 1.2

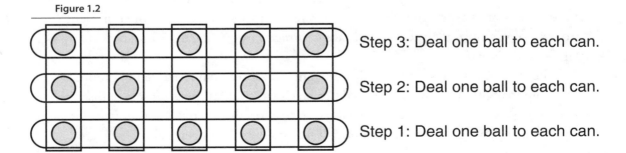

Step 3: Deal one ball to each can.

Step 2: Deal one ball to each can.

Step 1: Deal one ball to each can.

Multiplication as Iterating Numbers

Students begin to develop an understanding of multiplication by iterating (repeating and accumulating) numerical composite units. (A *composite unit* is a collection of things that has been mentally combined and treated as a unit.) For instance, to find the total in 5 groups of 3, we can create five instances of the composite 3 then count all the objects by ones (see Figure 1.3).

A more sophisticated way of solving this problem is to enumerate subtotals after each iteration by skip-counting (3, 6, 9, 12, 15). Iteration 1 gives the total in 1 composite of 3, iteration 2 gives the total in 2 composites of 3, iteration 3 gives the total in 3 composites of 3, and so on. The successive totals in enumerating composites of 3 are the skip-counts of 3.

Figure 1.3

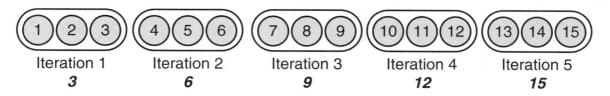

Multiplication as Coordinated Counting

To use iterative reasoning for multiplication, students must be able to coordinate simultaneous counting sequences—one for the number of objects in a group, one for the number of groups, and one for the total number of objects in accumulating iterations of groups. For example, to enumerate 5 groups of 3, a student might think, *1, 2, 3 (that's 1 group); 4, 5, 6 (that's 2 groups); 7, 8, 9 (that's 3 groups); 10, 11, 12 (that's 4 groups), 13, 14, 15 (that's 5 groups).* The student is coordinating the count for the total number of objects (1–15), the count for the number of groups (1 group, 2 groups,… 5 groups), and the count of 3 in each group (1, 2, 3 for objects in the first group; 4, 5, 6 for objects in the second group; and so on).

Coordinating these counting sequences is difficult, and lack of coordination is a major source of student errors. Indeed, as the factors get larger, it becomes more and more difficult for students to keep track of these counting sequences. So, for larger numbers, students need to move on to more sophisticated strategies for thinking about iteration and multiplication.

Relationship Between Multiplication and Division

In addition to understanding the various meanings of multiplication and division, students must also understand the critically important inverse relationship between multiplication and division. One way of expressing this inverse relationship is:

$$a \div b = c \quad \text{if and only if} \quad a = b \times c$$

Multiplication:	factor 1	×	factor 2	=	product
	3	×	5	=	15
Division:					
(multiplication language)	product	÷	factor 2	=	factor 1
	dividend	÷	divisor	=	quotient
(division language)	15	÷	5	=	3

Another way of expressing that multiplication and division are inverse operations is:

$$(n \times a) \div a = n \quad \text{or} \quad (n \div a) \times a = n$$

This expression shows that multiplication and division "undo" each other. If we start with 3 and multiply by 5, we get 15. To undo the effect on 3 of multiplying by 5, divide 15 by 5 and we get back to 3.

A very useful consequence of the inverse relationship between multiplication and division is that we can solve division problems by solving related multiplication problems. For instance, to solve 45 ÷ 15, we can ask: What number *times* 15 gives 45? For this reason, and because multiplicative reasoning is often easier than division reasoning, CBA-based instruction often emphasizes multiplication over division.

To further illustrate the inverse relationship and how we can replace division with multiplication, suppose students solve the problem 7 × 12 by skip-counting forward: 12, 24, 36, 48, 60, 72, 84. We might then pose the related division problem: How many 12s are in 84? Students might use the same skip-count sequence they used to find 7 × 12 to find 84 ÷ 12. Seven iterations of 12 produced 84, so 84 ÷ 12 = 7. Note that the numbers in this skip-count sequence are the sums resulting from repeatedly adding 12.

Another way to find 84 ÷ 12 is to skip-count by 12 backward from 84—72, 60, 48, 36, 24, 12, 0. Note that the numbers in this backward skip-count sequence are the differences produced by repeatedly subtracting 12 from 84. This is a difficult strategy to use, so CBA doesn't emphasize it. Because of the inverse relationship between multiplication and division, we can always replace backward skip-counting for division with forward skip-counting in the related multiplication problem.

We might visualize the relationship between multiplication and division in different contexts with the following table:

Multiplication	forward skip-counting	repeated addition
Division	backward skip-counting	repeated subtraction

Starting with Single-Digit Multiplication and Division

Because students must develop a good deal of proficiency with single-digit (SD) multiplication and division before progressing to multidigit (MD) multiplication and division, in Cognition-Based Assessment (CBA), we first examine levels of sophistication in students' reasoning about single-digit multiplication and division, along with instructional suggestions for helping students move through these levels. We then examine levels of sophistication in students' reasoning about multidigit multiplication and division and relevant instruction for this reasoning.

Importantly, before students progress to multidigit multiplication and division, they should develop sufficient fluency with the "basic facts" for multiplication and division (in CBA, the basic multiplication facts are problems that involve products of 2 *single-digit* numbers). Without adequate fluency with these facts, the cognitive demands required to implement multidigit multiplication and division will be too great for most students to handle. For instance, suppose students attempt to find 6×17 by multiplying 6 times 10, then 6 times 7, then adding the products. If they have to determine either 6×10 or 6×7 by counting by ones or skip-counting instead of quickly recalling either product, they will probably lose track of where they are in the overall computation because the brain's "working memory" is limited.

Nevertheless, students do not need complete mastery of basic facts before they can make sense of multidigit strategies. Students who know or can quickly derive most of their basic facts can reasonably start exploring multidigit problems. In fact, the distinction between single-digit and multidigit reasoning is not clear cut. For instance, students who regularly use skip-counting to determine products involving single digits often start to use skip-counting for simple multidigit problems like 6×12.

Multiplication Before Division

Although reasoning about multiplication generally develops before reasoning about division, students can often learn both operations at the same time. For example, after students become fluent at one CBA level of multiplication reasoning, they can begin solving division problems requiring that same level of reasoning. Other times, it makes more sense to stick with one operation for several levels. For instance, once students become fluent with multidigit multiplication at Level 3, it makes most sense for students to move next to Level 4 for multidigit multiplication.

Understanding Algorithms

The levels of sophistication in CBA describe students' development of core concepts and ways of reasoning about multiplication and division. An important part of this development is understanding and becoming fluent with using computational algorithms. *However, if algorithms are taught too early in students' development of reasoning about multiplication and division, students cannot understand the algorithms conceptually, so they learn them by rote.* Indeed, most students in traditional instruction learn traditional algorithms for multiplication and division by rote without understanding the underlying number properties. Chapter 2 contains a special section on understanding and determining levels of sophistication in students' use of computational algorithms.

Understanding Students' Levels of Sophistication for Multiplication and Division

The CBA approach to teaching students to multiply and divide whole numbers is built around detailed descriptions of levels of reasoning that allow us to tailor our instruction to meet students' learning needs. At first glance, the amount of detail can be overwhelming. So, keep in mind that understanding CBA levels develops in stages and over time. First, focus on learning the major features of the levels. Then, as you use CBA with your students, you will learn the finer details of the CBA framework.

Zooming Out to Get an Overview

To get an idea of the overall organization of the levels, examine the following "zoomed-out" view of the major ways students think about multiplication and division. Familiarize yourself with these major levels first without worrying about the sublevels that are discussed in Chapter 2.

SD Level 0	Student does not understand multiplication and division situations.
SD Level 1	Student multiplies or divides numbers by counting objects in groups by ones with no skip-counting.
SD Level 2	Student multiplies or divides numbers by repeated addition/subtraction or skip-counting.
SD Level 3	Student multiplies or divides numbers by recalling facts or by using properties to derive answers from known facts with no counting or skip-counting.
MD Level 1	Student multiplies or divides numbers by counting objects in groups by ones with no skip-counting.

MD Level 2	Student multiplies or divides numbers by repeated addition/subtraction or skip-counting.
MD Level 3	Student multiplies or divides numbers by using properties to combine or separate parts with no counting or skip-counting.
MD Level 4	Student uses and understands expanded multiplication and division algorithms.
MD Level 5	Student uses and understands traditional multiplication and division algorithms.

In the top row of this zoomed-out view, SD Level 0, students do not understand the concepts of multiplication and division. In the bottom two rows, MD Levels 4 and 5, students develop understanding of and fluency with algorithms for multiplication or division, first with expanded algorithms then with traditional algorithms.

In between the top and the bottom rows, students start with counting-based procedures for multiplying and dividing, first by ones then using skip-counting. Then students move to sophisticated, property-based, noncounting procedures that prepare them for deep conceptual understanding of computational algorithms. Roughly the same progression applies, first for single-digit numbers then for multidigit numbers:

Level 1: Students treat numbers as collections of ones (e.g., to find 7 × 5, the student makes 7 piles of 5 objects and counts them all as ones).

Level 2: Students use skip-counting to iterate composite units (e.g., to find 7 × 5, the student skip-counts 5 seven times—5, 10, 15, 20, 25, 30, 35).

Level 3: Students use known facts and number properties instead of counting (e.g., to find 7 × 5, the student reasons that 5 × 5 is 25, and 2 × 5 is 10, so 7 × 5 is 25 + 10 = 35).

Zooming In to Meet Individual Students' Needs

Understanding individual students' reasoning precisely enough to maximize their learning or remediate a learning difficulty requires a more detailed picture. We must zoom in to see CBA sublevels (see Figure 1.4). The jumps between sublevels must be small enough that students can achieve them with small amounts of instruction in relatively short periods of time.

Imagine students trying to climb the plateaus in the cognitive terrain described by CBA levels. In situation A, the student has to make a cognitive jump that is too great. In situation B, the student can get from Level 1 to Level 2 by using accessible sublevels as stepping-stones. To provide students with the instructional guidance and cognitive support they need to develop a thorough understanding of mathematical ideas, you need to understand and use the sublevels. Chapter 2 provides detailed descriptions and illustrations of all the CBA levels and sublevels for multiplication and division.

Figure 1.4 Accessible Cognitive Jumps

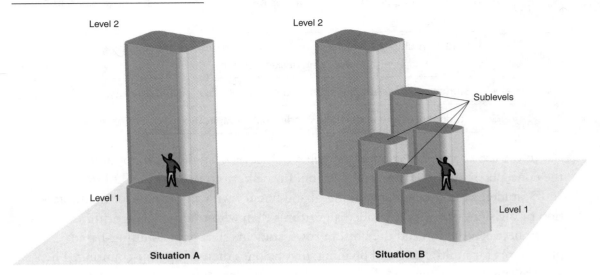

Level 2

Level 2

Sublevels

Level 1

Level 1

Situation A

Situation B

Chapter 2

Levels of Sophistication in Student Reasoning: Multiplication and Division

$$\times \div$$

The CBA approach to guiding students' development of understanding of multiplication and division builds on the CBA levels of sophistication in students' reasoning. Understanding these levels allows teachers to tailor instruction to meet students' individual learning needs. The major CBA levels (Levels 0, 1, 2, 3, 4, 5) provide an overview of the ways that students think about multiplying and dividing numbers. These levels describe how students progress from beginning understanding of multiplication and division concepts to meaningful use of multiplication and division algorithms.

Understanding students' reasoning precisely enough to maximize their learning or remediate their learning difficulties, however, requires a more detailed picture than is provided by the major levels, so the major levels are divided into sublevels. The "jumps" between sublevels are small enough that students can achieve them with small amounts of instruction in relatively short periods of time. Sublevels serve as accessible stepping-stones in students' development.

The following chart summarizes the CBA levels for multiplication and division. The following pages provide a detailed description of each level along with examples of student work at each level. At first glance, the amount of detail in the CBA levels can be overwhelming. So, keep in mind that understanding CBA levels develops in stages as you study examples of students' work and as you use CBA with your students.

Multiplying and Dividing Single-Digit Numbers			
Level	**Sublevel**	**Description**	**Page**
SD0		**Student does not understand multiplication or division situations.**	13
SD1		**Student multiplies or divides numbers by counting objects in groups by ones with no skip-counting.**	14
	1.1	Student counts physical or visual objects by ones.	14
	1.2	Student correctly counts visualized objects or counting words by ones.	16
	1.3	Student uses uncoordinated, incorrect skip-counting.	17
SD2		**Student multiplies/divides numbers by repeated addition/ subtraction or skip-counting.**	18
	2.1	Student uses repeated addition or subtraction, or skip-counts *and* counts by ones.	19
	2.2	Student decomposes a number into parts and skip-counts those parts.	20
	2.3	Student skip-counts all multiples in the skip-count sequence without decomposing numbers into parts.	21
	2.4	Student skip-counts a group of skip-counts.	22
SD3		**Student multiplies or divides numbers by recalling facts or by using properties to derive answers from known facts with no counting or skip-counting.**	23
	3.1	Student directly recalls basic multiplication or division facts.	23
	3.2	Student uses number properties to derive answers from known facts.	24

Level	Sublevel	Description	Page
Multiplying and Dividing Multidigit Numbers			
MD1		**Student multiplies or divides numbers by counting objects in groups by ones with no skip-counting.**	27
	1.1	Student counts physical or pictorial objects by ones (but not using place-value blocks).	27
	1.2	Student correctly counts groups of counting words by ones.	28
	1.3	Student uses uncoordinated and/or incorrect skip-counting.	29
	1.4	Student iterates multidigit numbers with place-value blocks, but still operates on the blocks as ones.	30
MD2		**Student multiplies or divides numbers by repeated addition/ subtraction or skip-counting.**	32
	2.1	Student uses repeated addition or subtraction or some counting by ones.	32
	2.2	Student skip-counts nonplace-value parts or a group of skip-counts.	34
	2.3	Student skip-counts all numbers in the skip-count sequence without decomposing numbers into parts.	38
	2.4	Student skip-counts by place-value parts.	40
MD3		**Student multiplies or divides numbers by using properties to combine or separate parts with no counting or skip-counting.**	43
	3.1	Student uses known multiplication or division facts and number properties to derive answers but does not use the distributive property with place-value decompositions.	44
	3.2	Student uses the distributive property to decompose numbers by place value into two partial products.	47
	3.3	Student uses the distributive property to decompose numbers by place value into four partial products.	50
MD4		**Student uses and understands expanded multiplication and division algorithms.**	52
MD5		**Student uses and understands traditional multiplication and division algorithms.**	59

Notes

1. To simplify the descriptions in this book, the discussion focuses only ones and tens in two-digit numbers. Similar, but more complicated, ideas occur for numbers containing more than two digits.

2. Implementing reasoning strictly verbally is more sophisticated than implementing it concretely or pictorially. Consequently, when investigating students' CBA levels, we should always determine and note if students need visible/physical material to implement their reasoning. So, for instance, if a CBA assessment task does not provide visual/physical material and students request it, ask them if they can do the problem without the material. Then let them check their answers with the material to see whether their answers are correct or not.

3. At certain times in students' learning, it can be helpful for them to use place-value blocks. But be careful about how you and students verbally refer to these blocks; the numerical value, not the shape, should be prominent. For instance, refer to the blocks below as follows.

"one" or "one-block" not "cube"	"ten" or "ten-block" not "strip" or "long"	"hundred" or "hundred-block" not "flat"

Also, the goal in using place-value blocks is to help students develop reasoning about numbers, not blocks. For instance, having students learn that 23 × 3 can be found by joining 3 copies of the place-value block representation 23, without understanding specifically how this representation is related to manipulations of numbers, is unlikely to be productive for students. In fact, it's important that when representing, say, 23 with place-value blocks, students recognize that the numeral 2 and the 2 ten-blocks both represent 2 tens or 20.

SINGLE DIGIT LEVELS

SD LEVEL 0: Student Does Not Understand Multiplication or Division Situations

Students do not understand multiplication and division situations, and so they inappropriately operate on the numbers given in the problem. Often, students' lack of comprehension is due to the fact that they do not understand that groups of objects, not just single objects, can be counted.

EXAMPLES

Task: *How many groups of 2 squares are there?*

Response: 1, 2, 3, 4, 5, 6.

This student counts individual objects rather than groups of objects.

Task: *Jon has 5 cans of tennis balls. Each can has 3 balls in it. How many tennis balls does Jon have altogether?*

Response: I'd say 8.

This student uses the wrong operation, adding instead of multiplying the numbers.

Task: *Jon has 15 tennis balls. If he puts 3 tennis balls in each can, how many cans does he need?*

Response: 3.

This student uses a number given in the problem as the answer.

Task: *Jon has 15 tennis balls. If he puts the same number of tennis balls in each of 5 cans, how many balls will be in each can?*

Response: *[Draws 5 circles]* I would put 5 in this one, and 5 in this one, and 3 in this one, and 1 in this one, and 1 in this one.

This student does not understand the idea of distributing objects into *equal* groups.

For strategies to help students at SD Level 0, see Chapter 3, page 72.

SD LEVEL 1: Student Multiplies or Divides Numbers by Counting Objects in Groups by Ones with No Skip-Counting

Students understand multiplication situations as determining the total number of objects in a set of equal groups by counting all objects in all groups *by ones*. Students understand division situations as using counting *by ones* to determine the number of objects in each equal group or the number of groups if the total is divided evenly into groups.

Sublevels depend on the representations students need to count objects by ones. At Level 1.1 students correctly solve problems only if they use physical or visual materials. At Level 1.2, students correctly solve problems using counting words (perhaps using fingers to keep track of the number of groups, but not ones within groups). At Level 1.3, students try to skip-count, but they make errors.

SD Level 1.1   Student counts physical or visual objects by ones.

Students form equal groups *of things that they can touch or see*. They act out the problem physically or visually. They count the total number of objects in all groups by ones. If students do not use physical or visual materials, they make mistakes in counting.

EXAMPLES

....

Task: $6 \times 8 =$

Response: I made 6 piles of 8 cubes. 1, 2, 3, 4, 5 . . . 46, 47, 48.

The student uses cubes to model the problem and counts all the cubes by ones.

....

Task: *I have 3 containers. There are 4 cubes in each container. How many cubes are there altogether?*

Response: *[Draws picture shown below]* I did 4 squares plus 4 squares plus 4 squares; then I am going to count them altogether. . . . 1, 2, 3, 4, 5, 6, 7, 8, 9, 10, 11, 12. [She writes "=12" to the right of the squares she drew.]

This student draws representations of the 3 sets of cubes then counts squares by ones to find the total.

Task: *I have 18 cubes. I want to put them into 3 containers. Each container must have the same number of cubes in it. How many cubes should be in each container?*

Response: Let's pretend these are the containers. *[Draws 3 containers. Says and writes the numbers 1 through 18.]* I wrote all of the numbers going up to 18; 18 is how many cubes. One goes here, one goes here, one goes here. *[Draws paths from 1, 2, and 3 to each of three containers, repeats until all 18 numbers are linked to containers.]* So, then you count how many lines go to the container, 1, 2, 3, 4, 5, 6. Then count if that's the same for all of them. 1, 2, 3, 4, 5, 6; 1, 2, 3, 4, 5, 6. *[Points to each path as he counts.]* Yeah, so there's 6 for each container.

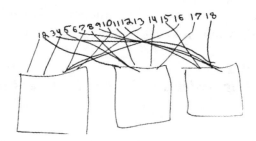

This student uses drawing to act out dealing the 18 numbers to each of 3 containers then counts the number of "lines" drawn to each container.

Task: *There are 3 cubes in each of these containers. Find the number of cubes in 4 containers.*

Response 1: Student empties the first container, counts 1, 2, 3 then taps 3 times on the top of the remaining containers as she counts 4, 5, 6; 7, 8, 9; 10, 11, 12.

This student counted imagined cubes in the remaining containers *after* she had actually counted the cubes in one container.

Response 2: 1, 2, 3 *[extending one finger]*; 4, 5, 6 *[extending a second finger]*; 7, 8, 9 *[extending a third finger]*; 10, 11, 12 *[extending a fourth finger]*; 13, 14, 15. There's 15. *[Teacher: Why did you stop at 15?]* Because that is the answer I got.

This student demonstrates a common error made by students at Level 1.1 when they do not use visual or physical materials. The student lost track of the number of containers.

Response 3: 1, 2, 3 *[extending one finger]*; 4, 5, 6 *[extending a second finger]*; 7, 8, 9, 10 *[extending a third finger]*; 11, 12, 12, 13 *[extending a fourth finger]*. There's 13.

In another common error made by students at this level, while counting, this student confused her count of cubes with her count of containers. When she counted 7, 8, 9, 10, she counted the 4 for the number of containers instead of the 3 for the number of cubes in a container.

Task: $4 \times 9 =$

Response: Count 4, 9 times. Four; 5, 6, 7, 8 *[counting on 4 fingers]*; 9, 10, 11, 12 *[counting on 4 fingers]*; 13, 14, 15, 16 *[counting on 4 fingers]*; 17, 18, 19, 20 *[counting on 4 fingers]*; 21, 22, 23, 24 *[counting on 4 fingers]*; 25, 26, 27, 28 *[counting on 4 fingers]*; 29, 30, 31, 32 *[counting on 4 fingers]*; 33, 34, 35, 36 *[counting on 4 fingers]*; 37, 38, 39, 40 *[counting on 4 fingers]*. *[Teacher: How did you know when to stop?]* I kept the 9 in my head. When I got close to 9, I sort of slowed down.

This student unsuccessfully tried to count groups of 4 mentally, using fingers to count the units in each group.

The last three examples illustrate that when students at Level 1.1 try to count counting words (as they would in Level 1.2), they lose track of objects or groups.

For strategies to help students at SD Level 1.1, see Chapter 3, page 73.

SD Level 1.2 Student correctly groups and counts imagined objects or counting words by ones.

Instead of using physical objects or drawings, students correctly form and count equal groups of imagined (visualized) objects or counting words. Students may use physical materials or fingers to represent the number of groups but not the objects within groups. For example, students might use four containers or four fingers to represent four groups. But they would not need to see the objects within the containers.

In Level 1.2, students must not only produce counting words, but they must also form equal groups of these counting words. Simultaneously producing and grouping counting words is more difficult than grouping physical objects or objects in pictures. One way that students make the transition to this more abstract setting is to raise fingers for the groups. Another way they make this transition is to visualize objects while they are counting. But it is usually difficult to know whether students are visualizing objects or just counting count words.

EXAMPLES

Task: $6 \times 8 =$

Response: *[Taps on the desk 8 times in the configuration below]* 1, 2, 3, 4, 5 … 8 *[holds up finger on one hand]*. *[Taps in the same configuration]* 9, 10, 11 … 16 *[puts up a second finger]*. *[Does this a total of 6 times]* … 47, 48.

This student counts counting acts (taps) for each group of 8, using fingers to keep track of the number of groups.

Task: *How many cubes are in 5 stacks of 3?*

Response: 1, 2, 3 *[extends one finger]*; 4, 5, 6 *[extends a second finger]*; 7, 8, 9 *[extends a third finger]*; 10, 11, 12 *[extends a fourth finger]*; 13, 14, 15 *[extends a fifth finger]*.

This student recognizes, keeps track of, and counts 5 groups of 3 counting-by-ones words. It is important to note that this kind of counting can be a critical precursor to skip-counting because students are *recognizing the skip-count words within the count-by-ones sequence*. While counting by ones, this student recognizes that saying 3 represents 1 group, saying 6 represents 2 groups, and so on.

Task: *I have 20 cubes. I want to put them into containers so there are 5 cubes in each container. How many containers do I need?*

Response: 1, 2, 3, 4, 5 *[raises one finger]*; 6, 7, 8, 9, 10 *[raises a second finger]*; 11, 12, 13, 14, 15 *[raises a third finger]*; 16, 17, 18, 19, 20 *[raises a fourth finger]*. *[Looking at raised fingers]* 4 containers.

This student used fingers to represent each group of 5 numbers as she counted to 20. Another student might perform the same actions and counting but visualize a particular spatial configuration of 5, such as the 5-dot side of a die.

For strategies to help students at SD Level 1.2, see Chapter 3, page 74.

SD Level 1.3 Student uses uncoordinated, incorrect skip-counting.

Students skip-count incorrectly because they cannot simultaneously keep track of (coordinate) the two counting schemes, one for the number of groups and one for the total number of objects in the groups.

EXAMPLE

Task: *I have 4 containers. There are 3 cubes in each container. How many cubes are there altogether?*

Response: 1 group is 3 *[puts up one finger]*, 2 groups is 6 *[puts up a second finger]*, 7 *[puts up a third finger]*, 8 *[puts up a fourth finger]*.

This student lost track of where he was in his simultaneous counting of number of objects and number of groups. He knew that he needed four counts (he raised four fingers). As shown below, his first two counts correctly skip-counted objects in groups by 3—"3, 6." But then he switched his last two counts to the count-by-ones sequence for number of groups—"7, 8."

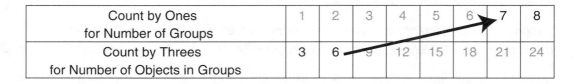

Count by Ones for Number of Groups		1	2	3	4	5	6	7	8
Count by Threes for Number of Objects in Groups	3	6	9	12	15	18	21	24	

For strategies to help students at SD Level 1.3, see Chapter 3, pages 74 and 75.

SD LEVEL 2: Student Multiplies or Divides Numbers by Repeated Addition/Subtraction or Skip-Counting

Repeated addition and subtraction and skip-counting are two efficient methods for multiplying and dividing single-digit numbers. Students should understand both methods. But as the sublevels of Level 2 indicate, there are several steps to gaining proficiency with these methods.

When students first start skip-counting a given number, they often know the first few skip-count numbers, but they are unfamiliar with later numbers in the skip-count sequence. To find the unknown numbers, students typically count on by ones or use repeated addition to continue the sequence. Also, when skip-counting a number, students frequently need to use fingers or tally marks to keep track of the number of repetitions of the number.

Level 2 contains four sublevels, but only Levels 2.1 and 2.3 should be major goals for teaching. Although some students may use Level 2.2 and 2.4 reasoning as they gain skip-count fluency, these levels are not a prerequisite for making progress toward Level 3.

Meaningful Skip-Counting

Students skip-count meaningfully when they understand that skip-counting is a shortcut for counting the objects in several equal groups by ones. For example, students might find the total in 4 equal groups of 5 objects by skip-counting 5 four times: 5, 10, 15, 20. This skip-count is meaningful if students understand that one group of 5 is 5, two groups of 5 are 10, three groups of 5 are 15, and four groups of 5 are 20.

To successfully skip-count objects by 5, students must coordinate two counting schemes, one for the number of groups of 5 and one for the total number of objects in successive groups of 5.

Number of Groups	1	2	3	4
Total Number of Objects in Groups	5	10	15	20

To see how skip-counting can be used for division, consider the problem 20 ÷ 5. To find the answer to 20 ÷ 5, students can skip-count backward: 20; 15, 10, 5, 0 (or 15, 10, 5, 0). Since it takes 4 backward skip-counts to get from 20 to 0, the quotient is 4. Note that because backward skip-counting is difficult, CBA instructional materials do not specifically teach this strategy. (Because of the difficulty of skip-counting backward, students often solve division problems by skip-counting forward.)

Using Repeated Addition and Subtraction to Multiply and Divide

As shown below, to use addition to find the product 4 × 5 (4 repetitions of 5), students can repeatedly add 5, keeping track of the number of 5s they add. Two 5s are added in the first problem and one 5 in each of the second two problems (making a total of four 5s).

$$
\begin{array}{ccc}
5 & 10 & 15 \\
+\,5 & +\,5 & +\,5 \\
\hline
10 & 15 & 20
\end{array}
$$

As shown next, repeated subtraction can be used to solve the division problem 20 ÷ 5 (how many 5s are in 20?). Because four 5s were subtracted, 4 is the answer.

$$
\begin{array}{cccc}
20 & 15 & 10 & 5 \\
-\,5 & -\,5 & -\,5 & -\,5 \\
\hline
15 & 10 & 5 & 0
\end{array}
$$

SD Level 2.1 Student uses repeated addition or subtraction, or skip-counts *and* counts by ones.

To multiply or divide numbers, students either repeatedly add or subtract all numbers in the sequence, or they skip-count some numbers then switch to repeated addition/subtraction or counting by ones to find the remaining numbers.

EXAMPLES

....

Task: *I have 4 containers like this. There are 3 cubes in each container. How many cubes are there altogether?*

Response 1: *[Extends one finger]* 3; *[extends another finger]* 6; *[extends another finger]* 9; *[extends another finger]* 10, 11, 12. 12 cubes.

This student skip-counts part of the skip-count-by-3 sequence then completes the sequence by counting by ones.

Response 2: I know that 3 + 3 is 6, then 3 + 3 is 6 again, so then I added the 6s together and got 12.

This student used repeated addition to find the total.

Task: *6 × 8 =*

Response: *[Writes successive addition problems]*

$$8 + 8 = 16$$
$$16 + 8 = 24$$
$$24 + 8 = 32$$
$$32 + 8 = 40$$
$$40 + 8 = 48$$

Let me check if I've added 8 six times [counts the 8s that appear in the addition problems]: 1, 2, 3, 4, 5, 6. It's 48.

This student used repeated addition by writing each addition problem separately.

Task: *I have 20 cubes. I want to put them in containers so there are 5 cubes in each container. How many containers do I need?*

Response: *[The student writes successive subtraction problems, talking as he writes.]*

20 – 5 =15. That's 1 container.
15 – 5 = 10. That's 2 containers.
10 – 5 = 5. That's 3 containers.
5 – 5 = 0. That's 4 containers.

I subtracted five 4 times, so there are 4 containers.

This student used repeated subtraction for division.

For strategies to help students at SD Level 2.1, see Chapter 3, page 75.

SD Level 2.2 Student decomposes a number into parts and skip-counts those parts.

Because students don't know the skip-count sequence for a number, they decompose the number into parts then skip-count the parts. These parts are numbers the students are more comfortable skip-counting, such as 2, 3, or 5. Sublevel 2.2 is not a proper goal for instruction because, although it involves clever reasoning, it is complex for students to manage without making errors.

EXAMPLE

Task: $6 \times 8 =$

Response: 5, 10, 15, 20, 25, 30 plus 3, 6, 9, 12, 15, 18. 30 plus 18 is 48.

Because this student could not skip-count by 8, he decomposed 8 into 5 and 3 then skip-counted each of these easier numbers 6 times.

For strategies to help students at SD Level 2.2, see Chapter 3, page 75.

SD Level 2.3 Student skip-counts all multiples in the skip-count sequence without decomposing numbers into parts.

Students multiply or divide numbers by skip-counting all the numbers in the relevant portion of a skip-count sequence. They reliably keep track of the number of times they skip-count a number.

EXAMPLES

Task: *I have 4 containers like this. There are 3 cubes in each container. How many cubes are there altogether?*

Response 1: *[Writes 3 and 1 underneath, 6 and 2 underneath, and so on, as shown below]* I did 3, 6, 9, 12, and underneath I did 1, 2, 3, 4. There's 12 cubes in the containers.

$$3, 6, 9, 12$$
$$1, 2, 3, 4$$

This student explicitly coordinated the skip-counting sequence for 3 with the counting sequence for the number of repetitions of 3.

Response 2: I'll count by 3s four times: 3, 6, 9, 12. There are 12 cubes.

This student skip-counted by 3, keeping track of the number of groups in her head.

Task: *I have 20 cubes. I want to put them into containers so there are 5 cubes in each container. How many containers do I need?*

Response: *[Puts up one finger for each skip-count number]* 5, 10, 15, 20. So you need 4 containers.

Task: *I have 18 cubes. I want to put them into 3 containers. Each container must have the same number of cubes in it. How many cubes should be in each container?*

Response 1: *[Draws three rectangles]* There's three containers. If I give 1 cube to each container, that's 3 cubes. *[Puts up one finger at a time]* 3, 6, 9, 12, 15, 18. *[Looks at raised fingers]* So, there's 6 cubes in each container.

This student used fingers to keep track of the number of groups of 3 during skip-counting.

Task: $4 \times 9 =$

Response: *[Makes a tally mark for each multiple of 4]* 4, 8, 12, 16, 20, 24, 28 *[counts tally marks by ones aloud to 7]*, 32, then 36.

This student used tally marks to keep track of the number of skip-counts of 4.

Task: $38 \div 5 =$

Response: *[Raising fingers one at a time]* 5, 10, 15, 20, 25, 30, 35. Seven 5s and there's a remainder of 3.

For strategies to help students at SD Level 2.3, see Chapter 3, page 77.

SD Level 2.4 Student skip-counts a group of skip-counts.

Students shorten a skip-count procedure by combining a group of skip-counts of the original number then skip-counting this group. Although this procedure is quite clever, it is often difficult for students to keep track of what they are doing. So, it is not explicitly encouraged in CBA instructional suggestions.

EXAMPLES

Task: $9 \times 4 =$

Response: 4, 8, 12; that's three 4s. Three more 4s would be 24; and three more 36.

This student skip-counted the first three numbers in the skip-count-by-4 sequence then skip-counted by 12 to find the total (recognizing that each skip-count by 12 was equal to 3 skip-counts of 4).

Task: *I have 20 cubes. I want to put them into containers so there are 5 cubes in each container. How many containers do I need?*

Response: You count by 5s: 5, 10, that's two 5s in 10. And two 10s in 20. So, you need 4 containers.

This student skip-counted two 5s to get 10 then recognized that two 10s equal 20, all the while keeping track of how many groups of 5 he counted.

For strategies to help students at SD Level 2.4, see Chapter 3, page 77.

SD LEVEL 3: Student Multiplies or Divides Numbers by Recalling Facts or by Using Properties to Derive Answers from Known Facts With No Counting or Skip-Counting

Students directly recall meaningful known multiplication/division facts, or they use number properties to derive answers from known facts. They do not count by ones, skip-count, or use repeated addition or subtraction.

A fact is *meaningful* (rather than rote) only if the student can justify the fact by counting, using physical/pictorial materials, or deriving the fact from other facts. So, when students recall known facts to determine if the fact is meaningful, you should ask questions such as: *How would you convince another student that 5 × 3 is 15?* Of course, once you establish that a student knows his or her facts meaningfully, you do not need to continue asking such questions.

SD Level 3.1 Student directly recalls basic multiplication or division facts.

Students directly recall a memorized fact.

EXAMPLES

Task: *I have 4 containers. There are 3 cubes in each container. How many cubes are there altogether?*

Response 1: 4 times 3 equals 12. *[Teacher: How did you get 12?]* See, if you do this, 4 + 4 + 4 equals 12 *[writing addition problem vertically]*. *[Teacher: Did you add like this?]* No, I just knew 4 times 3 is 12.

$$4 \times 3 = 12$$

$$\begin{array}{r} 4 \\ + 4 \\ 4 \\ \hline 12 \end{array}$$

This student knew and was able to justify with repeated addition the multiplication fact "4 times 3 equals 12."

Response 2: Twelve. I knew there's four containers and there's three cubes. And you would times 4 by 3 and I know that 4 by 3 is 12. *[Teacher: How do you know that?]* Because 3, 6, 9, 12—that's 4 threes.

This student knew the fact and could justify it by skip-counting.

....

Task: *I have 20 cubes. I want to put them into containers so there are 5 cubes in each container. How many containers do I need?*

Response: 20 divided by 5 equals 4. *[Teacher: How do you know?]* Well, 4 groups of 5 equals 20, so the answer's 4.

....

Task: *38 ÷ 5 =*

Response: Well, 7 times 5 equals 35, and there's a remainder of 3.

....

For strategies to help students at SD Level 3.1, see Chapter 3, page 78.

....

SD Level 3.2 Student uses number properties to derive answers from known facts.

At Level 3.2, students use known multiplication or division facts and number properties to derive answers. The number properties students use are illustrated in the following chart. Students generally do not know the name for the properties or their symbolic/algebraic formulations, but they have learned intuitively from experience the different valid ways that numbers can be multiplied and divided.

Property	Example	Algebraic Representation
Commutative Property of Multiplication (Division is not commutative.)	$3 \times 4 = 4 \times 3$	$a \times b = b \times a$
Inverse Relationship Between Multiplication and Division	$12 \div 4 = 3$ if and only if $4 \times 3 = 12$	$a \div b = c$ if and only if $b \times c = a$
Associative Property of Multiplication (Division is not associative.)	$5 \times 6 = 5 \times (2 \times 3)$ $= (5 \times 2) \times 3$ $= 10 \times 3$	$a \times (b \times c)$ $= (a \times b) \times c$
Division/Multiplication Property	$42 \div 6 = 42 \div (2 \times 3)$ $= (42 \div 2) \div 3$ $= 21 \div 3 = 7$	$a \div (b \times c)$ $= (a \div b) \div c$
Distributive Property for Multiplication	$7 \times 8 = 7 \times (5 + 3)$ $= (7 \times 5) + (7 \times 3)$ $= 35 + 21 = 56$ or $(4 + 3) \times 8$ $= (4 \times 8) + (3 \times 8)$	$a \times (b + c)$ $= (a \times b) + (a \times c)$ or $(a + b) \times c$ $= (a \times c) + (b \times c)$
Distributive Property for Division	$45 \div 5 = (20 + 25) \div 5$ $= (20 \div 5) + (25 \div 5)$ $= 4 + 5 = 9$	$(a + b) \div c$ $= (a \div c) + (b \div c)$

EXAMPLES

Task: *What is 5 groups of 3?*

Response: Three groups of 3 is 9, and 2 more groups of 3 is 6, and $9 + 6 = 15$.

This student uses an intuitive version of the distributive property:

$$5 \times 3 = (3 + 2) \times 3 = (3 \times 3) + (2 \times 3)$$

Task: $6 \times 8 =$

Response: 5 times 8 is 40, plus 1 more 8 is 48.

This student uses an intuitive form of the distributive property:

$$6 \times 8 = (5 + 1) \times 8 = (5 \times 8) + (1 \times 8)$$

Task: *8 × 13 = 104; what is 9 × 13?*

Response: 8 times 13 is 104; 9 times 13 would mean you'd have to add another 13 to 104, because 9 is 1 more than 8. *[Adds as shown, getting 117]:*

$$9 \times 13 = \underline{ 117 }$$

$$\begin{array}{r} 104 \\ +13 \\ \hline 117 \end{array}$$

This is another example of using the distributive property.

Task: *I have 20 cubes. I want to put them into containers so there are 5 cubes in each container. How many containers do I need?*

Response: 20 divided by 5. Division is just multiplication backward. So, if you know multiplication, you know division; 5 times 4 equals 20 *[writes 5 × 4 = 20]*, so 20 divided by 5 is 4.

This student derives a division fact from a multiplication fact using the inverse relationship between multiplication and division.

Task: *7 × 14 = 98; what is 14 × 7 = ?*

Response: *[Almost immediately]* 98. It's sort of the same thing. It's just reversed.

This student uses the commutative property of multiplication.

Task: *I have 24 pieces of candy. I want to put them into 6 bags so that there is the same number of candies in each bag. How many candies should I put in each bag?*

Response: 12 divided by 6 equals 2. Another 12 divided by 6 equals another 2. So, it's 2 plus 2 equals 4 candies in a bag.

Task: *4 × 9 = ?*

Response: 2 times 9 is 18, and 2 times 18 is 36.

This student uses the associative property of multiplication.

For strategies to help students move to the initial stages of multidigit multiplication and division, see Chapter 4, page 86.

MULTIDIGIT LEVELS

MD LEVEL 1: Student Multiplies or Divides Numbers by Counting Objects in Groups by Ones with No Skip-Counting

When multiplying and dividing multidigit numbers, students treat the numbers exclusively as *collections of ones*. They count the total number of objects in the groups by ones. If skip-counting is used, it is used incorrectly. When students first multiply and divide multidigit numbers, they often return to the physical/visual methods they initially used with single-digit numbers (often with the use of base-ten blocks).

The sophistication of students' reasoning in MD Level 1 depends on the types of representations students need. At Level 1.1, students can correctly solve problems only if they use physical or visual materials. At Level 1.2, students can correctly solve problems using only counting words (perhaps using fingers to keep track of the number of groups, not ones within groups). At Level 1.3, students try to skip-count, but they make errors in coordinating the count-by-ones sequence for number of groups and the skip-count sequence for the total number of objects in the groups. At Level 1.4, students represent multidigit numbers with base-ten blocks or base-ten drawing but still operate on tens and ones as ones.

MD Level 1.1 Student counts physical or pictorial objects by ones (but not using place-value blocks).

Students form equal groups *out of things they can see or touch*. They have to act out the problem physically or visually. They count the total number of objects in the groups by ones. If students do not use physical or visual material, they make mistakes in counting.

EXAMPLES

Task: *I have 6 plates of cookies. There are 23 cookies on each plate. How many cookies are there altogether?*

Response: *[Student draws 6 circles]* There's 6 plates. *[Student draws 23 tally marks in each circle]* Put 23 cookies in each. Count all the cookies: 1, 2, 3 … 137, 138.

This student drew a picture to represent and count all the cookies on the plates by ones. (Students who use the same strategy but miscount are also at Level 1.1 but functioning at a slightly lower level within Level 1.1.)

Task: *48 divided by 4*

Response: *[Student partitions 48 cubes into 4 equal groups by dealing cubes to groups one at a time]* One for you, one for you, one for you, one for you ... *[After no cubes are left, student counts the cubes in one group]* 1, 2, ... 11, 12.

This student used a physical representation.

Task: *Find the number of cubes in 12 containers, with 4 cubes in each container.*

Response: *[Student draws 12 squares then taps 4 times in each]* 1, 2, 3, 4; 5, 6, 7, 8; ... 45, 46, 47, 48.

This student used a pictorial representation combined with tapping to count the objects in 12 containers by ones.

For strategies to help students at MD Level 1.1, see Chapter 4, page 86.

MD Level 1.2 Student correctly counts groups of counting words by ones.

Instead of using physical or visualized objects, students determine the result of multiplying or dividing by counting *groups of counting words*. Students at this level may use fingers to represent the number of groups but not units within groups. Students do not draw groups or units within groups.

EXAMPLES

Task: *A carton contains 12 eggs. Emily has 5 cartons. How many eggs does Emily have altogether?*

Response 1: 1, 2, 3 ... 11, 12 *[puts up one finger]*; 13, 14 ... 23, 24 *[puts up another finger]*; ... 48, 49 ... 59, 60 *[puts up a fifth finger]*. 60 eggs.

Response 2: 1, 2, 3, 4, 5 *[puts up one finger]*; 6, 7, 8, 9, 10 *[puts up another finger]*; ... 46, 47, 48, 49, 50 *[puts up a tenth finger then puts all 10 fingers down]*; 51, 52, 53, 54, 55 *[puts up one finger for 11]*; 56, 57, 58, 59, 60 *[puts up a second finger for 12]*. 60 eggs.

Student 1 recognizes, keeps track of, and counts 5 groups of 12 counting-by-ones words. Student 2 recognizes, keeps track of, and counts 12 groups of 5 counting-by-ones words.

Task: *I have 55 cubes. I want to put them into containers so there are 11 cubes in each container. How many containers do I need?*

Response: 1, 2, 3, 4, 5, 6, 7, 8, 9, 10, 11 *[raises one finger]*; 12, 13, 14, 15, 16, 17, 18, 19, 20, 21, 22 *[raises a second finger]*; 23, 24, 25, 26, 27, 28, 29, 30, 31, 32, 33 *[raises a third finger]*; 34, 35, 36, 37, 38, 39, 40, 41, 42, 43, 44 *[raises a fourth finger]*; 45, 46, 47, 48, 49, 50, 51, 52, 53, 54, 55 *[raises fifth finger]*. *[Looking at her 5 raised fingers]* You need 5 containers.

Like the student in the first example, this student uses fingers to keep track of groups of counting-by-ones words.

Task: *Mary has 84 cookies. She wants to divide them equally among 4 people. How many cookies does each person get?*

Response: 1, 2, 3, 4 *[raises one finger]*; 5, 6, 7, 8 *[raises a second finger]*; 9, 10, 11, 12 *[raises a third finger]* … 37, 38, 39, 40 *[raises a tenth finger then puts all 10 fingers down]*; 41, 42, 43, 44 *[raises one finger for 11]*; … 77, 78, 79, 80 *[raises a tenth finger for 20 then puts all 10 fingers down]*; 81, 82, 83, 84 *[raises one finger for 21]*. I did 21 fingers; so it's 21 cookies for each person.

This student uses fingers to determine how many groups of 4 are in 84. Note that each group of 4 can be thought of as dealing one round of cookies to 4 people.

For strategies to help students at MD Level 1.2, see Chapter 4, page 87.

MD Level 1.3 Student uses uncoordinated and/or incorrect skip-counting.

Mental skip-counting of multidigit numbers taxes students' mental processing capacity. Consequently, while attempting to skip-count, students lose track of the two counting schemes, one for the number of groups and one for the total number of objects in the groups (their coordination of these two counting schemes breaks down).

EXAMPLES

Task: *3 × 26*

Response: 26, 46, 52.

This student improperly conceptualizes how to skip-count by 26. She first adds the 20 from 26 to 26 to get 46 then she adds the 6 from 26 to 46 to get 52. Although 52 is the second skip-count number for 26, because she performs two steps to get 52 from 26, she thinks that 52 is the third skip-count number for 26.

Task: *5 × 13*

Response: 13, 26, 31, 36, 41.

This student loses track of what he is skip-counting. He starts skip-counting by 13 but then switches to skip-counting by 5.

For strategies to help students at MD Level 1.3, see Chapter 4, page 87.

MD Level 1.4 Student iterates multidigit numbers with place-value blocks, but still operates on the blocks as ones.

Students use place-value blocks to represent multidigit numbers. But they don't fully understand the relationship between tens and ones, so they may still count only by ones. Or they may translate place-value blocks into numbers without fully understanding the translation. For example, students might say that 3 ten-blocks is thirty *without counting* "ten, twenty, thirty" or without being able to give any other justification for their claim.

EXAMPLES

Task: *3 × 26*

Response 1: *[Student gathers 3 sets of 2 ten-blocks and 6 one-blocks.]*

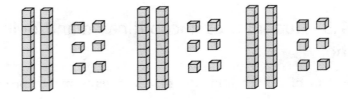

Three groups of 26. *[Counts all cubes in the blocks by ones]* 1, 2, 3 … 78.

This student appropriately represents two-digit numbers with place-value blocks, but he does not treat the tens as tens when he counts.

Response 2: *[Student gathers 3 sets of 2 ten-blocks and 6 one-blocks then groups the ten-blocks together and the one-blocks together.]*

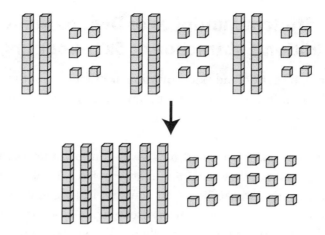

[Pointing at the 6 tens] 60; *[pointing at the ones]* 61, 62, 63 . . . 78.

[Teacher: How do you know that these 6 ten-blocks are sixty?] Because I just know that 6 of these is sixty.

This student identifies the six tens as 60 (without justification) then counts on by ones.

Task: *Mary has 84 cookies. She wants to divide them equally among 4 people. How many cookies does each person get?*

Response: *[Student makes 84 from 8 ten-blocks and 4 one-blocks]* Give one of these to each person *[deals out 4 ten-blocks]*. Give one more to each person *[deals out 4 more ten-blocks]*. Now each person gets one of these *[one-blocks]*. So, each person gets 21.

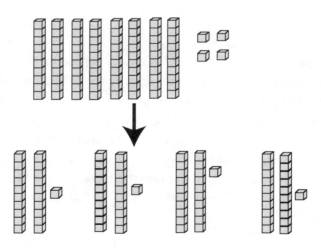

This student distributes the tens and ones separately.

For strategies to help students at MD Level 1.4, see Chapter 4, page 88.

MD LEVEL 2: Student Multiplies or Divides Numbers by Repeated Addition/Subtraction or Skip-Counting

Repeated addition/subtraction and skip-counting are two efficient methods for multiplying/dividing multidigit numbers. Students should understand both methods. But as the sublevels of Level 2 indicate, there are several steps to gaining proficiency with these methods.

When students first start skip-counting a given number, they often know the first few skip-count numbers, but they are unfamiliar with later numbers in the skip-count sequence. To find the unknown numbers, students typically count on by ones or use repeated addition to continue the sequence. Also, when skip-counting a number, students frequently need to use fingers or tally marks to keep track of the number of repetitions of the number.

Level 2 contains four sublevels, but only Levels 2.1, 2.3, and 2.4 should be major goals for teaching. Although some students may use Level 2.2 reasoning as they gain skip-count fluency, this level is not a prerequisite for making progress toward Level 3.

Note 1

Although repeated addition/subtraction and skip-counting are valid ways to multiply and divide numbers (and are more efficient than counting all by ones), these methods can be tedious and error-prone if at least one of the factors is not reasonably small. We should not expect students to become proficient in using these methods when both numbers are multidigit.

Note 2

Although using repeated subtraction and backward skip-counting are valid ways to perform division, these methods are definitely more difficult for students than repeated addition and forward skip-counting. Consequently, for division problems, students often use repeated addition and forward skip-counting to solve a multiplication problem that is related to the given division problem. However, although use of backward skip-counting for division is a legitimate strategy for students, using repeated subtraction should be a goal because the recommended expanded algorithm for division is based on repeated subtraction.

MD Level 2.1   Student uses repeated addition or subtraction or some counting by ones.

Students either (a) use repeated addition or subtraction to multiply or divide numbers or (b) skip-count a couple of numbers then switch to repeated addition or subtraction or counting by ones to find the unknown numbers in the skip-count sequence.

EXAMPLES

Task: *There are 32 chairs in a classroom. Each chair has 4 legs. How many chair legs are there in the classroom?*

Response: If I do 4, 32 times, that's gonna take a long time. So, I'm gonna do 32 times 4. So *[writing as shown below]* I will do 32 plus 32; that's 64. Plus another 32 equals 96; plus another 32 equals 128. We have one, two, three, four 32s—we're gonna have 128 legs.

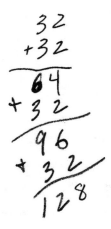

This student uses the commutative property and repeated addition to find the product.

Task: *96 ÷ 24 =*

Response: 24 is one *[writes 24 and 1 under it]*. 48 *[writes 48 and 2 under it]*. *[Counting on from 48 to 68, first by twenty then by ones]* 48, 68; 69, 70, 71, 72. *[Counting 24 more beyond 72 by tens and ones]* 72, 82, 92; 93, 94, 95, 96.

$$24, 48, 72, 96$$
$$1 \quad 2 \quad 3 \quad 4$$

This student counts on by tens and ones to perform the repeated addition.

Task: *There are 32 chairs in a classroom. Each chair has 4 legs. How many chair legs are there in the classroom?*

Response: Add 32 four times. *[Writes the problem 32 + 32 + 32 + 32 vertically and uses the traditional addition algorithm.]* 2 + 2 + 2 + 2 is 8. And 3 + 3 + 3 + 3 is 12. *[Writes 128 as answer.]*

$$
\begin{array}{r}
32 \\
32 \\
32 \\
32 \\
\hline
128
\end{array}
$$
legs
chairs

This student uses a traditional addition algorithm to perform repeated addition.

Task: *There are 180 sticks in bundles of 12. How many bundles are there?*

Response: Using paper and pencil, student repeatedly subtracts 12, starting at 180, and continues to subtract until he arrives at zero. He then counts how many subtractions he did, getting 15.

This student recognizes that he can subtract to find the answer and is able to count the number of subtractions required.

For strategies to help students at MD Level 2.1, see Chapter 4, page 91.

MD Level 2.2 Student skip-counts nonplace-value parts or a group of skip-counts.

Students decompose a number into nonplace-value parts then skip-count the parts or skip-count a group of skip-counts.

Nonplace-Value Parts

Students decompose numbers into smaller parts that they can skip-count more easily, but they do not use place-value parts.

Task: *Roberto made 4 plates of cookies. There were 23 cookies on each plate. How many cookies were there altogether?*

Response: 21, 42, 63, 84. Plus, 2, 4, 6, 8. So, that's 84 plus 8 equals 92.

This student decomposed 23 into 21 and 2 then skip-counted each part. (Students who skip-count 20, 40, 60, 80, then 3, 6, 9, 12, then add 80 and 12 are *skip-counting place-value parts*.)

Task: *Ron has 4 bags of 28 candies. How many candies does he have altogether?*

Response: 25, 50, 75, 100. Plus, 3, 6, 9, 12. Ron has 112 candies.

A Group of Skip-Counts

Students shorten a skip-count procedure by combining a group of skip-counts of the original number then skip-counting this group. Sometimes students combine skip-counts into unequal sums that they can easily add. Other times students combine skip-counts of the original number into a larger number then skip-count the larger number. Either way, however, it can be difficult for students to keep track of the skip-counts of the original number.

EXAMPLES

Task: $20 \times 8 =$

Response: I know that 20 + 20 is 40, and I add 40 more and I get 80; then I add 80 more, 80 + 80, and get 160. *[Teacher: How many 20s does that give you?]* I know that 40 is two 20s, 80 is four 20s, and 160 is eight 20s.

This student combines skip-counts of 20 into larger numbers using a doubling strategy, all the while keeping track of how many skip-counts of the original number (20) have occurred, quite a feat of mental processing.

Task: *There are 32 chairs in a classroom. Each chair has 4 legs. How many chair legs are there in the classroom?*

Response: *[Saying and writing]* 4, 8, 12, 16, 20, 24, 28, 32, 36, 40 *[then writing 1, 2 … 9, 10 underneath the skip-counted numbers].* For every 10, I have 40. Instead of going farther, I would go 40, 80, 120 *[holds up 3 fingers]*, so we know 30 chairs is 120 so far. Plus 2 more chairs would be 128 legs.

$$4, 8, 12, 16, 20, 24, 28$$
$$1, 2, 3, 4, 5, 6, 7$$

$$32, 36, 40$$
$$8, 9, 10$$

This student's short-cut for skip-counting 4 thirty-two times is to skip-count 4 ten times to make 40 then to skip-count 40 three times, keeping track that skip-counting 40 is the same as skip-counting 10 fours. He then adds 8 for the 2 in 32. The method is correct and quite sophisticated.

Task: *48 ÷ 4 =*

Response: Four 4s is 16. Add another 16 is 32; that would be eight 4s. Add another 16 and I would get 48. So, I would have twelve 4s *[writes 12 in the answer space].*

$$4 \times 4 = 16$$
$$8 \quad 32$$
$$12 \quad 48$$

This student skip-counts groups of four 4s.

Task: *256 ÷ 8 =*

Response: Two 8s is 16; two 16s is 32; so right now, I would have four 8s *[writing 4 next to 32].* And 64's another four 8s; that's eight 8s *[writing 8 next to 64].* *[Writes]* 128, that's four more 8s. If I double 128, I'll get 256, then I'll double that *[12]* and get 24.

$$32 \quad 4$$
$$64 \quad 8$$
$$128 \quad 12$$
$$256 \quad 24$$

This student loses track of what he is doing during his short-cut process. When he doubled the 64, he should have doubled the 8 to get 16, not added 4 to get 12.

....

Task: *9 × 13 =*

Response: First I would add 9 three times. *[Writes 9 three times vertically]* 9, 18, 27 *[writes 27]*. Then another 27 *[writes 3 more 27s]*. There are four 27s, and that would equal 12 *[groups of 9]*. So, I would add another 9 *[writes 9 under the four 27s then adds using the traditional addition algorithm]*. 117.

This student adds 3 nines to make 27. He then writes three more 27s to make four 27s and understands that this is 12 nines. Because he wants 13 nines, he adds another 9 to the list. Finally, he adds 27 + 27 + 27 + 27 + 9 using the traditional addition algorithm to get 117.

Task: *Matt has 120 cubes. He wants to put the cubes into bags, with 15 cubes in each bag. How many bags does he need?*

Response: I do division I think. I think I am going to have to add. *[She writes 15 four times and adds them, getting 60. She then adds another 60 to the first 60 and gets 120.]* It can go in 8 times.

[Teacher: How did you get that?]

I did 15 + 15 + 15 + 15 and it was 60. Then I added 60 + 60 and I got 120.

[Teacher: How do you know that is 8 times?]

15 + 15 + 15 + 15 is 60. That's 4 right there. Plus another 60, that would be another 4 more. 60 + 60 is 120 and 4 + 4 is 8.

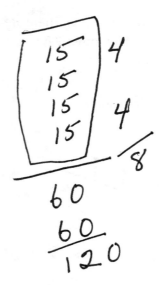

This student added four 15s to make 60 and added two 60s to make 120. She understood that her additions amounted to eight 15s. Although she computed her additions mentally, she needed to write what she was doing to keep track of it.

For strategies to help students at MD Level 2.2, see Chapter 4, page 91.

MD Level 2.3 Student skip-counts all numbers in the skip-count sequence without decomposing numbers into parts.

Students skip-count all numbers in a skip-count sequence. They do not decompose numbers into parts.

EXAMPLES

Task: *5 × 13*

Response: 13, 26, 39, 42, 55.

This student seems to understand how to skip-count by 13; however, she makes an error when trying to find the skip-count after 39, no doubt because of the required regrouping.

Task: *A carton contains 12 eggs. Emily has 5 cartons. How many eggs does Emily have altogether?*

Response: I'll count by 12s. 12, 24, 36, 48, 60 *[keeping track of her 5 counts of 12 on her fingers]*. So, there's 60 eggs.

This student correctly skip-counts by 12.

Task: *10 × 6 =*

Response: I just know that 10 six times is 10, 20, 30, 40, 50, then 60.

This student, like many students, is comfortable skip-counting by 10.

Task: *Mary has 84 cookies. She wants to divide them equally among 4 people. How many cookies does each person get?*

Response: Try giving each person 20; that's 20, 40, 60, 80. No, I'm not giving each person enough. Try 21; 21, 42, 63, 84. So, 21 works. Give each person 21 cookies.

This student estimates the quotient, checks her estimate by skip-counting, adjusts her estimate, then checks the new estimate by skip-counting.

Task: *Matt has 120 cubes. He wants to put the cubes into bags, with 15 cubes in each bag. How many bags does he need?*

Response: Start with 120, count 15 back, that's 105 *[puts up one finger]*, 90 *[puts up a second finger]*, 75 *[puts up a third finger]*, 60 *[puts up a fourth finger]*, 45 *[puts up a fifth finger]*, 30 *[puts up a sixth finger]*, 15 *[puts up a seventh finger]*, 0 *[puts up an eighth finger]*. He needs 8 bags.

This student correctly skip-counts 15 backward from 120 using fingers to keep track of the number of skip-counts.

For strategies to help students at MD Level 2.3, see Chapter 4, page 92.

MD Level 2.4 Student skip-counts by place-value parts.

Students skip-count by place-value parts. For instance, consider 4 × 23; the place-value parts of 23 are 20 in the tens place and 3 in the ones place. To skip-count 23 by its place-value parts: skip-count by 20; 20, 40, 60, 80; skip-count by 3; 3, 6, 9, 12; then add 80 and 12 to get 92. Or skip-count the tens part by individual tens; 10, 20; 30, 40; 50, 60; 70, 80 (keeping track that you need two 10-counts to make a 20-count; skip-count the ones part; 3, 6, 9, 12; then add 80 and 12 to get 92. Sometimes students skip-count the ones part, starting at the end of the skip-count of the tens part. For example, for 4 × 23, the student skip-counts by 20; 20, 40, 60, 80; then skip-count by 3, starting with 80; 83, 86, 89, 92.

Using Visual Materials

Some students need physical or visual representations of place-value blocks to implement skip-counting multidigit numbers by place-value parts.

EXAMPLES

Task: *3 × 26*

Response 1: *[Student gathers 3 sets of 2 ten-blocks and 6 one-blocks.]*

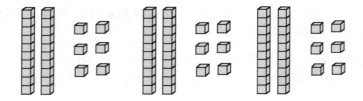

Three groups of 26. 10, 20, 30, 40, 50, 60. 6, 12, 18. 78.

This student skip-counted the individual tens in the tens part 20, skip-counted the ones, then added the two results.

Response 2: *[Student gathers 3 sets of 2 ten-blocks and 6 ones.]*

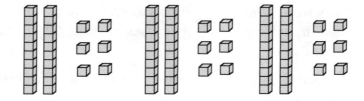

20, 40, 60; 66, 72, 78.

This student skip-counts the tens part 20 then skip-counts the ones. Unlike the first student, this student counts on rather than counting the tens and ones separately.

Response 2 is more sophisticated than Response 1 because Response 2 skip-counts the whole tens part, not the tens within it.

Task: *124 ÷ 4*

Response: I'm gonna use blocks. *[Gets 12 ten-blocks as she skip-counts]* 10, 20, 30, 40, 50, 60, 70, 80, 90, 100, 110, 120, and 4 *[gets 4 one-blocks]*.

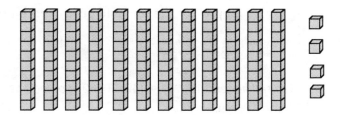

I'm gonna put these in 4 groups *[draws 4 loops on an extra large piece of construction paper]*. Put 1 ten in each group; that's 10, 20, 30, 40. Put another ten in each group; that's 40 more. Put another ten in each group; that's 40 more. So, that's 40, 80, 120 so far. Then put 1 in each group; that's 124. So, there's 10, 20, 30, 31 in each group *[pointing to the blocks in one group]*.

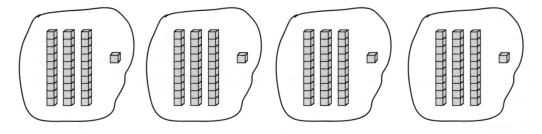

This student partitions tens and ones separately into 4 equal groups, then skip-counts by tens and ones to find the number in each group.

Not Using Visual Materials

Skip-counting by place-value parts without place-value blocks is more abstract, difficult, and sophisticated than using blocks.

EXAMPLES

Task: *Mary has 84 cookies. She wants to divide them equally among 4 people. How many cookies does each person get?*

Response: *[As she draws the following]* I put 10 in each group, that's 40; then 10 more in each, that makes 80; then 1. So, each person gets 21 cookies.

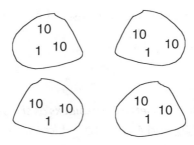

This student writes numerals to represent the tens and ones in each group.

Task: *6 × 13 =*

Response: *[Looking at 6 raised fingers]* 10, 20, 30, 40, 50, 60. *[Looking at 6 raised fingers]* 3, 6, 9, 12, 15, 18. Add 60 and 18, equals 78.

This student skip-counts the tens and ones separately and adds the results.

Task: *48 ÷ 4*

Response: *[Putting up four fingers]* 10, 20, 30, 40. *[Putting up four fingers]* 2, 4, 6, 8. So, 10 plus 2 works.

The student distributes the tens part 40 into 4 groups of 10 then the ones part 8 into 4 groups of 2.

Task: *Roberto made 6 plates of cookies. There were 23 cookies on each plate. How many cookies were there altogether?*

Response 1: 10, 20 *[raises a finger]*; 30, 40 *[raises a second finger]*; 50, 60 *[raises a third finger]*; 70, 80 *[raises a fourth finger]*; 90, 100 *[raises a fifth finger]*; 110, 120 *[raises a sixth finger]*. 3, 6, 9, 12, 15, 18. 120 plus 18 equals 138.

This student counts the tens and ones separately, using fingers to keep track of the number of groups of 2 tens, then adds the results.

Response 2: *[Raising a finger for each skip-count]* 20, 40, 60, 80, 100, 120. *[Looking at her six raised fingers]* 3, 6, 9, 12, 15, 18. 120 and 18 make 138 cookies.

This student skip-counts the whole tens part of 20 then skip-counts the ones.

Task: *There are 32 chairs in a classroom. Each chair has 4 legs. How many chair legs are there in the classroom?*

Response: *[Writes four 32s vertically and adds them using the traditional algorithm.]* I did 2, 4, 6, 8. That's 8. 30, 60, 90, 120. 128's the answer.

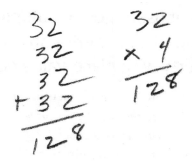

This student decomposed 32 into 2 and 30 and was able to skip-count each part then add the results to find the product.

For strategies to help students at MD Level 2.4, see Chapter 4, page 96.

MD LEVEL 3: Student Multiplies or Divides Numbers by Using Properties to Combine or Separate Parts With No Counting or Skip-Counting

Students determine problem solutions without skip-counting or counting by ones. Instead, they use various number properties to derive answers from other answers. At first, they use properties that are *unconnected* to place-value decomposition of numbers (a place-value decomposition of a number separates the number into its place-value parts; so 35 would be decomposed as 3 tens and 5 ones). Next, they use place-value decompositions coupled with the distributive property, first decomposing numbers into two partial products then into four partial products.

Important Note

Reasoning at MD Levels 3.2 and 3.3 is very similar to the reasoning in using expanded algorithms in MD Level 4. However, use of Levels 3.2 and 3.3 reasoning is *not* the same as use of an expanded algorithm because Levels 3.2 and 3.3 reasoning is impromptu and not always performed in exactly the same way (as is required for an algorithm). This is true even when students do some writing while implementing Levels 3.2 and 3.3 reasoning.

MD Level 3.1 Student uses known multiplication or division facts and number properties to derive answers but does not use the distributive property with place-value decompositions.

Students use known multiplication or division facts and number properties to derive answers. *However, students do not use the distributive property together with place-value decompositions at this level—that occurs at MD Level 3.2.*

The number properties students use are illustrated below. Students generally do not know the names for properties or their algebraic formulations. Instead, they have learned from experience the different valid ways that numbers can be manipulated. Often, students combine the properties below with knowledge that multiplication can be accomplished by repeated addition and division with repeated subtraction.

Property	Example	Algebraic Representation
Multiplication Can Be Done by Repeated Addition	$3 \times 4 = 4 + 4 + 4$	
Division Can Be Done by Repeated Subtraction	To find $12 \div 4$, count how many times 4 can be subtracted from 12.	
Commutative Property of Multiplication (Division is not commutative.)	$3 \times 4 = 4 \times 3$	$a \times b = b \times a$
Inverse Relationship Between Multiplication and Division	$12 \div 4 = 3$ if and only if $4 \times 3 = 12$	$a \div b = c$ if and only if $b \times c = a$
Associative Property of Multiplication (Division is not associative.)	$5 \times 6 = 5 \times (2 \times 3)$ $= (5 \times 2) \times 3$ $= 10 \times 3$	$a \times (b \times c)$ $= (a \times b) \times c$
Division/Multiplication Property	$140 \div 20 = 140 \div (10 \times 2)$ $= (140 \div 10) \div 2$ $= 14 \div 2$	$a \div (b \times c)$ $= (a \div b) \div c$
"0" Rule of Multiplication Example: To find 80×30, append two 0s to 8×3. This rule uses the associative and commutative properties and place value.	$80 \times 30 = (8 \times 10) \times (3 \times 10)$ $= (8 \times 3) \times (10 \times 10)$ $= 24 \times 100$ $= 2400$	$(a \times b) \times (c \times d)$ $= (a \times c) \times (b \times d)$

Cognition-Based Assessment and Teaching of Multiplication and Division

Property	Example	Algebraic Representation
Distributive Property for Multiplication	$7 \times 12 = 7 \times (6 + 6)$ $= (7 \times 6) + (7 \times 6)$ $= 42 + 42$ or $7 \times 12 = 7 \times (10 + 2)$ $= (7 \times 10) + (7 \times 2)$ $= 70 + 14$ or $7 \times 12 = (5 + 2) \times 12$ $= (5 \times 12) + (2 \times 12)$ $= 60 \times 24$	$a \times (b + c)$ $= (a \times b) + (a \times c)$ $(a + b) \times c$ $= (a \times c) + (b \times c)$
Distributive Property for Division	$95 \div 5 = (50 + 45) \div 5$ $= (50 \div 5) + (45 \div 5)$ $= 10 + 9 = 19$	$(a + b) \div c$ $= (a \div c) + (b \div c)$

EXAMPLES

In the first three examples, students use the "0" rule for multiplication to derive answers for problems involving multiples of ten from their related basic facts.

Task: $3 \times 40 =$

Response: I know that 3 times 40 = 120 because 3 times 4 equals 12.

Task: $10 \times 37 =$

Response: 370. You just add a zero.

Task: $10 \times 40 =$

Response: 400. If it would be 10 times 4, it would be 40. But you have this zero here, so that's one more zero, so that's 400.

Task: *5 × 12 =*

Response: *[Writes]* Add them and get 60.

$$5 \times 5 = 25$$
$$5 \times 5 = 25$$
$$5 \times 2 = \underline{10}$$
$$60$$

Task: *132 divided by 6*

Response: If I add 6 thirties, I'll get 180. So, 30 is too big. If I add 6 twenties, I'll get 120. So, 20 is too small. If I add 6 twenty-twos, I'll get 120 plus 12. So, 22 is the answer.

This student uses a combination of several properties: multiplication as repeated addition; the 0 rule of multiplication seems to be used to find 6 thirties; the distributive property is used to find 6 twenty-twos. It is the complexity of this computation that prevents it from being a Level 3.2 response.

Task: *Find 160 divided by 20.*

Response: There are five 20s in 100, and three 20s in 60, so there are eight 20s in 160.

Task: *There are 22 students. Each has 6 folders. How many folders are there altogether?*

Response: I remembered that 20 times 5 is 100. And 20 times 6 is 20 more; that's 120. Then add 2 more 6s. I got 132.

Task: *32 × 14 =*

Response: 10 times 14 equals 140; so, add 140 three times *[adds three 140s on paper, getting 420]*. Two times 14 is 28. So, it's 420 plus 28; 448.

Task: *132 ÷ 6 =*

Response: 120 divided by 6 is 20. 12 divided by 6 is 2. So, it's 22.

In the above four examples, students use various properties—the 0 rule for multiplication, multiplication as repeated addition, the inverse relationship between multiplication and division—in combination with implicit use of the distributive property.

Task: *140 ÷ 6 =*

Response: 120 divided by 6 is 20. 18 divided by 6 is 3. So, it's 23 remainder 2. *[Teacher: How can you check your answer?]* 6 times 23: 6 times 20 equals 120. 6 times 3 is 18. So, 6 times 23 equals 138. Then you add the remainder of 2 and you get 140.

For strategies to help students at MD Level 3.1, see Chapter 4, page 99.

MD Level 3.2 Student uses the distributive property to decompose numbers by place value into two partial products.

Students use the distributive property combined with place-value decomposition to calculate products and quotients of multidigit numbers. For instance, as shown below, to decompose the multiplication problem *5 × 32* using the distributive property and place value is to decompose the problem into $(5 \times 30) + (5 \times 2)$ because 32 is decomposed into its tens and ones parts.

$$5 \times 32 = 5 \times (30 + 2) = (5 \times 30) + (5 \times 2)$$

↑	↑
Decompose 32 into its "place-value parts" of tens and ones (30 and 2)	*Use distributive property. (5 × 30) and (5 × 2) are called "partial products."*

Two distributive-property decompositions of *5 × 32* that are *NOT* by place value are:

$$(5 \times 20) + (5 \times 12) \text{ and } (5 \times 10) + (5 \times 10) + (5 \times 2)$$

Decompositions using place value and the distributive property are particularly important because understanding them enables students to understand how computational algorithms for multiplication work.

Level 3.2 reasoning is easiest for students to implement when a two-digit number is multiplied by a one-digit number. But sometimes students attempt this kind of reasoning when multiplying 2 two-digit numbers.

EXAMPLES

Task: *5 × 32 =*

Response: 5 times 30 equals 150. And five 2s is 10. 160.

Task: *A carton contains 12 eggs. Emily has 5 cartons. How many eggs does Emily have altogether?*

Response: Five 10s is 50 *[writes]*. Five 2s equals 10 *[writes]*. 50 plus 10 equals 60 *[adding vertically and writing 60 underneath]*. So, the answer's 60.

$$5 \times 12 = 60$$

$$\begin{array}{r} 5 \times 10 = 50 \\ 5 \times 2 = \underline{+10} \\ 60 \end{array}$$

Task: *32 × 14 =*

Response: 3 times 14 equals *[pause]* 42; so, 30 times 14 is 420. Add 28, so it's 448.

Task: *10 × 37 =*

Response: 10 times 30 is 300; 10 times 7 is 70, and you have to add these two up and it is 370.

Task: *8 × 32 =*

Response: 8 times 30 and 8 times 2. It should be 240 and 16 *[writes]*; and if we add these up together, it is 256.

$$\begin{array}{r} 8 \times 30 = 240 \\ 8 \times 2 = \underline{+\ 16} \\ 256 \end{array}$$

Task: *There are 22 students. Each has 6 folders. How many folders are there altogether?*

Response: 20 times 6 equals 120. Then add 2 more 6s. I got 132.

Task: *132 divided by 6*

Response: 6 times 30 equals 180, so 30 is too big. 6 times 20 equals 120. The 12 left over divided by 6 equals 2. So, it's 22.

As shown below, Level 3.2 reasoning can also be used for some rather special division problems, with students sometimes using base-ten blocks to aid their reasoning.

Task: *128 ÷ 4*

Response 1: 100 divided by 4 equals 25. 20 divided by 4 equals 5. 8 divided by 4 equals 2. Add 25 plus 5 plus 2 equals 32. *[Decomposes 128 into hundreds, tens, and ones parts.]*

Response 2: 120 divided by 4 equals 30. 8 divided by 4 equals 2. So, the answer is 32. *[Decomposes 128 into tens and ones parts.]*

Response 3: 128 is 12 tens and 8 ones. *[Decomposes 128 into tens and ones parts.]*

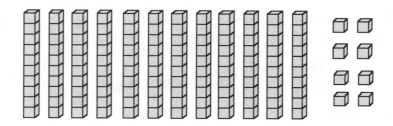

Response 4: Put the tens into 4 equal groups; 12 divided by 4 equals 3. That's 3 tens or 30 in each group. Put the ones into 4 groups; 8 divided by 4 equals 2. So, there's 32 in each group.

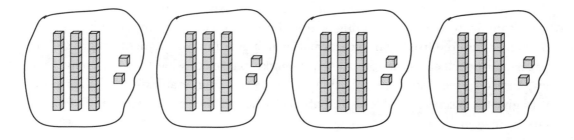

Note on Division

Level 3.2 reasoning can be reasonably applied in problems in which place value parts are each divisible by the divisor, like 488 ÷ 4 or 128 ÷ 4. More complicated problems like that below force students to use remainders, which is difficult to do correctly.

Task: *128 ÷ 8*

Response 1: 100 divided by 8 equals 12, remainder 4. 20 divided by 8 equals 2, remainder 4. 8 divided by 8 equals 1. Now put the two remainders together and divide 8 by 8, that's 1. So, 12 plus 2 plus 1 plus 1 equals 16.

Response 2: 100 divided by 8 equals 10, remainder 20. 20 in the remainder plus 20 in 128 makes 40. 40 divided by 8 equals 5. 8 divided by 8 equals 1. Add 10 plus 5 plus 1 equals 16.

Because of the complexity in such division problems, students are much more likely to be successful using multiplication to find these quotients.

For strategies to help students at MD Level 3.2, see Chapter 4, page 100.

MD Level 3.3 Student uses the distributive property to decompose numbers by place value into four partial products.

To find a product of 2 two-digit numbers, students decompose *both* two-digit numbers into two place-value parts then use the distributive property. For example,

$$25 \times 32 = (20 + 5) \times (30 + 2)$$
$$= (20 \times 30) + (20 \times 2) + (5 \times 30) + (5 \times 2)$$

The four place-value-based partial products are:

$$(20 \times 30), (20 \times 2), (5 \times 30), \text{ and } (5 \times 2)$$

Decomposing problems into four partial products is quite difficult for students to understand. But comprehending such decompositions is critical for students' *understanding* of algorithms for multiplication and division.

At MD Level 3.3, students do not use either an expanded or traditional algorithm. Instead, their reasoning is more impromptu and intuitive, and it is not organized into the fixed symbolic format of an algorithm. But students might still use paper-and-pencil computations to help them keep track of what they are doing. One way to determine if students are using Level 3.3 thinking or an expanded algorithm is to give them several problems and observe whether they always write their computations the same way.

EXAMPLES

Task: *25 × 14 =*

Response: *[Student writes and says the following:]*

20 times 10 is 20 tens; that would be 200.

20 times 4 equals 60.

5 times 10 is 50.

5 times 4 equals 20.

200 plus 60 plus 50 plus 20 equals 330.

$$25 \times 14 = 330$$

$$20 \times 10 = \cancel{201} \; 200$$
$$20 \times 4 = 60$$
$$5 \times 10 = 50$$
$$5 \times 4 = 20$$

$$200 + 60 + 50 + 20$$
$$330$$

This student decomposes 25 into 20 and 5 and 14 into 10 and 4 and adds the four partial products to find the total. Note that the student incorrectly multiplied 20 times 4, which caused his answer to be incorrect.

Task: $45 \times 34 =$

Response: [Student writes and says the following]:

30 times 40 is—3 times 4 is 12, add the two zeros—1200. 30 times 5 is 150 because 3 times 5 is 15 and add the zero. 40 times 4 is 160 because 4 times 4 is 16 and just add the zero. 4 times 5 is 20. Add them. 1200 plus 100 plus 100 equals 1400. 50 plus 60 plus 20 equals 140. 1400 plus 140 equals 1540.	$30 \times 40 = 1200$ $30 \times 5 = 150$ $40 \times 4 = 160$ $4 \times 5 = 20$ $\overline{1,540}$

This student correctly decomposes the problem into its four place-value-based partial products. But he adds the partial products incorrectly. Also note that the way he writes his partial products is not as nicely organized as the previous student. To be completely organized, he would have written 4 × 40 instead of 40 × 4.

As shown below, to apply the four-partial-product reasoning to division requires thinking of division in terms of multiplication (and is more difficult than dealing with multiplication). The following example illustrates the cleverness of this reasoning. However, this reasoning is, in general, too complex to make a goal for instruction.

Task: *910 ÷ 35*

Response: *[First, the student tries to find the tens digit of the quotient.]*

30 times 30 is 900; 30 times 5 is 150; that's 1050 altogether. So 30 is too big. I'll try 20.

20 times 30 is 600; 20 times 5 is 100; that's 700 altogether. 910 minus 700 equals 210. There's 210 left.

[Next, the student tries to find the ones digit of the quotient to see how many 35s are in 210.]

35 times 5 would be 150 plus 25, or 175. That's not enough. So, try 35 times 6.

35 times 6 would be 180 plus 30, which is 210. So, it's 6.
My answer is 20 plus 6, equals 26.

For strategies to help students at MD Level 3.3, see Chapter 4, page 103.

MD LEVEL 4: Student Uses and Understands Expanded Multiplication and Division Algorithms

At MD Level 4, students use and understand expanded computational algorithms for multiplying and dividing multidigit numbers. Expanded algorithms explicitly show the values of place-value part computations throughout the sequence of steps in the algorithms. Numbers are treated in their place-value "expanded" form; for example, 35 is treated as 30 + 5. In the language used to guide performance of the algorithm, the 3 in 35 is said "30," not "3." These expanded algorithms show the results of intermediate operations in their entirety. Generally, students learn algorithms for multiplication before those for division.

To gain understanding and fluency with expanded algorithms, students must not only understand relevant number properties, but they must also be fluent with mentally multiplying multiples of ten. One of the major reasons for using expanded algorithms is that these algorithms explicitly build on students' MD Level 3.3 reasoning. That is, once students are able to implement MD Level 3.3 reasoning, they should be encouraged to organize this reasoning into the fixed sequence of written steps of the expanded algorithms shown below. In addition to conceptually connecting algorithms with MD Level 3.3 reasoning, the use of expanded algorithms gives students a way to organize and make efficient their MD Level 3.3 reasoning. Without the practiced organization of expanded algorithms, many students who are capable of Level 3.3 reasoning get lost in the complexity of their computations. Fluent use of expanded algorithms reduces students' mental processing load as they perform computations, making it less likely that they will make errors.

To see the difference between Level 3.3 and Level 4 reasoning, consider the problem 25 × 14.

In both Levels 3.3 and 4 reasoning, students have to compute and add the following 4 partial products: 20 × 10, 20 × 4, 5 × 10, 5 × 4.

With Level 3.3 reasoning, students first must recognize that all four partial products are needed. Then students have to explicitly decide the order in which to compute the products (order doesn't matter), and they have to decide what to write as they do these computations. Some students write just the answers; others write each partial product and its answer. They need to decide whether to write the partial product computations horizontally or vertically. Finally, they have to use however they wrote the partial product answers to add them.

Using an expanded algorithm can greatly reduce the decisions that students need to make during this computation because the sequence of steps in the algorithm is memorized, thus reducing students' cognitive load. For instance, according to the fixed sequence in one expanded algorithm, the sequence of steps for this problem, and problems like it, is as follows:

$$
\begin{array}{r}
25 \\
\times\,14 \\
\hline
20 \\
80 \\
50 \\
\underline{200} \\
350
\end{array}
$$

Expanded Algorithms for Multiplication

Two examples of expanded algorithms for multiplication are illustrated below.

Problem and Written Solution	Multiplication Algorithm 1 (2-digit times 1-digit)	Multiplication Algorithm 1 (2-digit times 2-digit)	Multiplication Algorithm 2 (2-digit times 2-digit)
	$53 \times 4 = ?$ 53 $\times 4$ 12 200 212	$53 \times 24 = ?$ 53 $\times 24$ 12 4×3 200 4×50 60 20×3 1000 20×50 1272	$53 \times 24 = ?$ $(50 + 3)$ $\times (20 + 4)$ 4×3 12 4×50 200 20×3 60 20×50 1000 1272
What Student Says During Computation	4 times 3 is 12; write 12. 4 times 50 is 200; write 200. 200 plus 12 is 212.	4 times 3 is 12; write 12. 4 times 50 is 200; write 200. 20 times 3 is 60; write 60. 20 times 50 is 1000; write 1000. 12 plus 200 equals 212, plus 60 equals 272, plus 1000 equals 1272.	53 equals 50 plus 3. 24 equals 20 plus 4. 4 times 3 is 12; write 12. 4 times 50 is 200; write 200. 20 times 3 is 60; write 60. 20 times 50 is 1000; write 1000. Now add them up. 2 plus 0 plus 0 plus 0 equals 2. 10 plus 60 equals 70, write the 7. 200 write the 2. Plus 1000, write the 1. So, it's 1272.

Expanded Algorithms for Division

Below are two examples of expanded algorithms for division.

Problem and Written Solution	*Division Algorithm 1* (Less efficient method) $528 \div 7 = ?$ 7)528 −350 (50 × 7) 178 −140 (20 × 7) 38 −35 (5 × 7) 3 75 Answer: 75 remainder 3	*Division Algorithm 2* (Most efficient method) $528 \div 7 = ?$ 7)528 −490 70 38 −35 5 3 75 Answer: 75 remainder 3
What Student Says During Computation	*How many times can I subtract 7 from 528? (How many 7s are in 528?)* *Can I subtract 100 sevens? No.* *If I subtract 50 sevens, I am subtracting 350, with 178 left over.* *If I subtract 20 sevens from 178, I have 38 left over.* *If I subtract 5 sevens from 38, I have 3 left over.* *So, I have subtracted a total of 50 plus 20 plus 5 equals 75 sevens, and I have 3 left over as a remainder.*	*How many times can I subtract 7 from 528?* *Can I subtract 100 sevens? No.* *Can I subtract 70 sevens? Yes.* *Can I subtract 80 sevens? No.* *So subtract 70 sevens, that is, 490, with 38 left over.* *Subtract 5 sevens, and get 3 left.* *So, I have subtracted a total of 70 plus 5 equals 75 sevens, and I have 3 left over as a remainder.*

Task: *Mary has 84 cookies. She wants to divide them equally among 4 people. How many cookies does each person get?*

Response: *[Using Division Algorithm 1, the student writes and speaks as shown below.]*

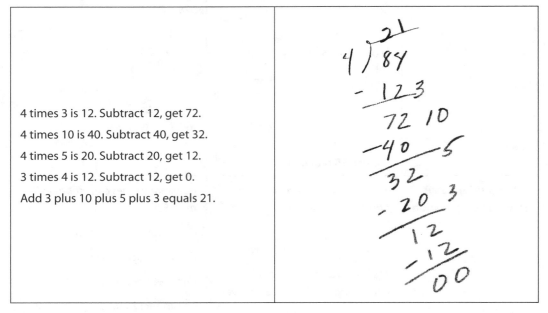

4 times 3 is 12. Subtract 12, get 72.

4 times 10 is 40. Subtract 40, get 32.

4 times 5 is 20. Subtract 20, get 12.

3 times 4 is 12. Subtract 12, get 0.

Add 3 plus 10 plus 5 plus 3 equals 21.

In using Division Algorithm 1, this student successively subtracted multiples of groups of 4, which she found manageable.

Task: *45 × 23 =*

Response: *[The student says and writes what is shown below.]*

3 times 5 equals 15.

3 times 40 equals 120.

20 times 5 equals 100.

20 times 40 equals 800.

Add them. 1035.

[Teacher: Why did you do 4 multiplications? Where are these numbers (points to 15, 120, 100, 800) coming from?]

Student. Well, you do 3 times 5, then 3 times 40, then 20 times 5, and 20 times 40. Then you add up all the parts.

This student uses Multiplication Algorithm 1 (in which only the answers to partial products are written). His answer to the teacher's question indicates that he understands the algorithm.

Task: *490 divided by 14*

Response: *[The student says and writes what is shown below.]*

14 times 10 equals 140. Subtract, equals 350. 14 times 10 equals 140. Subtract, equals 210. 14 times 10 equals 140. Subtract, equals 70. 14 times 5 equals 70. Add 3 tens and 5 equals 35.	$$\begin{array}{r} 14\overline{)490} \\ -140 \rightarrow 10\times14 \\ \hline 350 \\ -140 \rightarrow 10\times14 \\ \hline 1\,8\,4\,0 \\ -140 \rightarrow 10\times14 \\ \hline 7\,0 \\ -70 \rightarrow 5\times14 \\ \hline 0 \end{array}$$

In using Division Algorithm 1, this student successively subtracted groups of 14, which he found manageable.

....

Task: *161 ÷ 7 =*

Response: *[The student says and writes what is shown below.]*

7 times 10 is 70. 7 times 20 is 140. 7 times 30 is 210 is too big. So, it's 20 *[writes 7 × 20].* Subtract, get 21. 7 times 3 equals 21 *[writes 7 × 3].* Add 20 and 3; 23. [Teacher: So, what do the 20 and 3 mean?] The 20 means that we are using 20 groups of 7; then 3 groups of 7. That's how many groups of 7 there are. [Teacher: How can you be sure your answer is right?] I could multiply 7 times 23 and I should get 161. [Student does the multiplication to the right of the division problem.]	$$\begin{array}{r} 7\overline{)161} \\ -140 \quad 7\times20 \\ \hline 21 \\ -21 \quad 7\times3 \\ \hline 0 \end{array}$$ $$\begin{array}{r} 7\times23 \\ 20\times7 = 140 \\ 3\times7 = 21 \\ \hline 161 \end{array}$$

This student uses Expanded Division Algorithm 2. And her answers to the teacher's questions show that she understands the algorithm.

An Alternative Expanded Division Algorithm

The preceding expanded division algorithm is based on the measurement or repeated-subtraction interpretation of division (see Chapter 1). For instance, for 528 ÷ 7, we ask how many 7s are in 528. As shown previously, we can subtract groups of 7 in various ways.

A different expanded division algorithm is based on the partitive interpretation of division (see Chapter 1), which we can explain using place-value blocks. Using this second expanded algorithm, to divide 528 by 4, we *partition* the place-value block representation of 528 into 4 equal groups, as shown below. Note how the steps with base-ten blocks correspond to the steps in the traditional algorithm (shown in the left two columns).

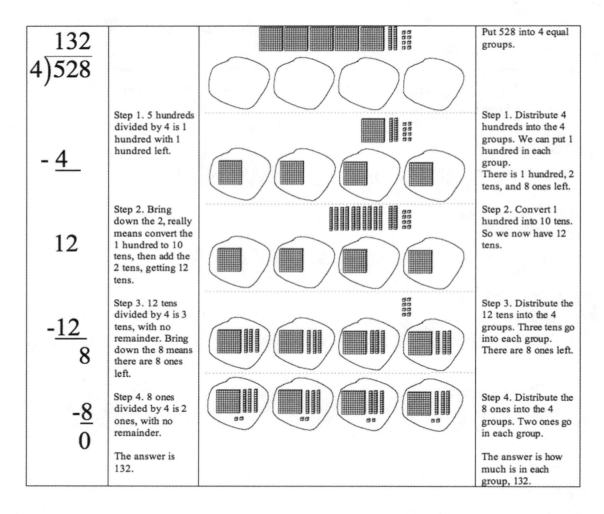

$$\begin{array}{r} 132 \\ 4\overline{)528} \end{array}$$	Put 528 into 4 equal groups.
Step 1. 5 hundreds divided by 4 is 1 hundred with 1 hundred left. $-\underline{4}$	**Step 1.** Distribute 4 hundreds into the 4 groups. We can put 1 hundred in each group. There is 1 hundred, 2 tens, and 8 ones left.
Step 2. Bring down the 2, really means convert the 1 hundred to 10 tens, then add the 2 tens, getting 12 tens. 12	**Step 2.** Convert 1 hundred into 10 tens. So we now have 12 tens.
Step 3. 12 tens divided by 4 is 3 tens, with no remainder. Bring down the 8 means there are 8 ones left. $\begin{array}{r} -\underline{12} \\ 8 \end{array}$	**Step 3.** Distribute the 12 tens into the 4 groups. Three tens go into each group. There are 8 ones left.
Step 4. 8 ones divided by 4 is 2 ones, with no remainder. $\begin{array}{r} -\underline{8} \\ 0 \end{array}$ The answer is 132.	**Step 4.** Distribute the 8 ones into the 4 groups. Two ones go in each group. The answer is how much is in each group, 132.

For strategies to help students at MD Level 4, see Chapter 4, page 107.

MD LEVEL 5: Student Uses and Understands Traditional Multiplication and Division Algorithms

Using their understanding of place value and other properties of numbers, as embodied in the expanded algorithms, students conceptually understand traditional algorithms for whole-number multiplication and division, even though the place-value ideas in these algorithms are hidden.

In addition to understanding numbers as combinations of their place-value parts, students understand and can move flexibly between various place-value part representations. For example, students understand that the 2 in 243 can be thought of as 200 ones, 2 hundreds, or 20 tens. This enables them to understand the regrouping processes ("carrying" and "borrowing") performed in the algorithm. Many students make sense of traditional algorithms by relating them step by step to expanded algorithms.

EXAMPLES

Task: *45 × 23 =*

Response:

[Writing as shown on the left] 3 times 5 is 15, write the 5, carry the 1 up here *[writes 1 above the 4]*. 3 times 4 is 12, plus 1 is 13 *[writes 13]*. 2 times 5 is 10, write the 0, carry the 1 *[writing 0 below the 3 in 135]*. 2 times 4 is 8, plus 1 is 9.

[Teacher: Is this 1 up here (pointing to the 1 from 15) really a 1?]

It's 10 from the 15.

[Teacher: Why did you write the 0 from 2 times 5 here (pointing)?]

Because it's really 20 times 5. Look, another way to do the problem is like this. *[Writes out the expanded algorithm shown at the right of the original problem.]* See, the top two numbers under 45 × 23 make 135; they come from 3 times 45, which is 40 + 5 *[brackets 15 and 120 and writes 135]*. And the bottom two numbers, the 100 and 800, make 900; they come from the 20 times 40 + 5 *[brackets them and writes 900]*. The 90 over here is really 900 over here [pointing first to the problem on the left and then to the one on the right].

This student refers to the expanded algorithm to justify the steps he used in the traditional algorithm, demonstrating that he understands the critical place-value concepts and number properties involved.

Task: *928 ÷ 4*

Response: *[After first using the standard algorithm (on the right), she uses an expanded algorithm.]* So, the 2 here above the 9 really means 200 because you're subtracting 200 fours, which is 800—and that's why you put minus 8 under the 9 hundred. It's the same for the 3 which is really 30 and 12 which is 120. And the 2 is really 2 and the 8 is really 8.

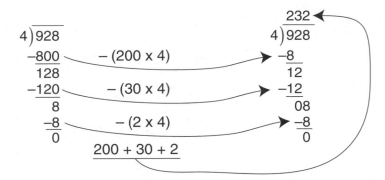

As with the multiplication example above, this student is able to use the expanded algorithm to demonstrate her understanding of the concepts underlying the traditional algorithm.

Students' Understanding of Algorithms

Even though students cannot conceptually understand multiplication and division algorithms until they reach MD Level 3, many curricula introduce these algorithms before students have developed Level 3 reasoning. This section describes students' understanding of these algorithms and how to assess it. As you will see, if students do not make errors in their computations, to determine the level of students' understanding of algorithms, it is critical that you ask appropriate questions. There are four types of understanding that students can exhibit for algorithms.

1. Students incorrectly perform an algorithm.

This is the easiest type of understanding to detect because students perform an algorithm incorrectly. They do not understand the steps in the algorithm or the underlying properties or place-value concepts.

EXAMPLES

Task: *45 × 34 =*

Response: *[Writes 34 times 45 vertically and begins to multiply digits, writing the products vertically.]* 5 times 4 is 20; 5 times 3 is 15; 4 times 3 is 12; and 4 times 4 is 16. Add them, 63.

$$
\begin{array}{r}
34 \\
\times\,45 \\
\hline
20 \\
15 \\
12 \\
+\,16 \\
\hline
63
\end{array}
$$

Task: *848 ÷ 8 =*

Response: 8 goes into 8 one time *[writes 1 above the left 8 in 848]*. Subtract 8 and get nothing. Bring down the 4. 8 does not go into 4, bring down the 8. 48 divided by 8 equals 6 *[writes the 6 next to the 1 above 848]*. 16.

$$
\begin{array}{r}
16 \\
8\,\overline{)848} \\
-8 \\
\hline
48 \\
-48 \\
\hline
0
\end{array}
$$

2. Students correctly perform an algorithm but with a clear indication that it is *not* understood.

Students correctly perform a symbolic algorithm, but there is a clear indication that they do not understand underlying properties or place-value concepts. This lack of understanding is generally uncovered only by questioning the student. Indeed, whenever students use language that ignores place value, you should query them about their understanding.

EXAMPLE

Task: *45 × 23 =*

Response: 3 times 5 is 15, put 5 here *[writes]*, carry the 1 up here *[writes 1 above 4]*. 3 times 4 is 12 plus 1 is 13 *[writes 13]*. 2 times 5 is 10, write the 0 *[under 3 in 135]*, carry the 1 *[writes another 1 above the 4]*. 2 times 4 is 8 plus 1 is 9.

$$
\begin{array}{r}
\overset{\scriptstyle 1}{4}5 \\
\times\ 23 \\
\hline
135 \\
90 \\
\hline
1035
\end{array}
$$

Note that the student's language does not refer to place value. For instance, when the student says, "3 times 4 is 12 plus 1 is 13," the proper language would be "3 times 40 equals 120, plus 10 more is 130." Because this student's language lacks proper place-value references, her teacher asks questions to probe her understanding of place-value principles in the algorithm. The student's answers give a clear indication that she does not understand these underlying principles.

Teacher: Is this 1 up here [pointing to the 1 from 15 directly above the 4 in 45] really a 1?

Student: Yes, it's from the 15.

Teacher: Why did you write the 0 from 2 times 5 here [pointing at 0 in 90]?

Student: Because you have to put it under the 3.

Teacher: Why do you have to put it under the 3?

Student: Because if you don't, you will get the wrong answer.

Task: *848 ÷ 8 =*

Response: 8 goes into 8, 1 time *[writes 1 above 8]*. Subtract 8, get 0. Bring down the 4. 8 does not go into 4 *[writes 0 next to 1]*, bring down the 8. 48 divided by 8 equals 6 *[writes the 6 next to the 0]*. 106.

$$
\begin{array}{r}
106 \\
8\,\overline{)848} \\
-8 \\
\hline
048 \\
-48 \\
\hline
0 \\
\end{array}
$$

Teacher: Why did you put the 1 above the 8?

Student: Because you put the first number on top over the first number in the division thingy.

Teacher: Why did you put the –8 over here?

Student: Because that's where you are supposed to put it.

Teacher: Why did you subtract 8?

Student: Because that is what you are supposed to do.

3. Students correctly perform an algorithm with no indication of understanding or misunderstanding.

Students correctly perform a symbolic algorithm, but there is no indication of understanding the underlying place-value concepts. That is, students might not understand the algorithm, or they might understand the algorithm but provide no evidence of this understanding. Only appropriate questioning can reveal students' understanding (see the teacher questions in the previous section). So in the example below, because there are no probing follow-up questions, we cannot determine if the student understands the underlying place-value principles.

EXAMPLE

Task: *45 × 23 =*

Response: 3 times 5 is 15, put 5 here *[writes]*, carry the 1 up here *[writes 1 above 4]*. 3 times 4 is 12 plus 1 is 13 *[writes 13]*. 2 times 5 is 10, write the 0 *[under 3 in 135]*, carry the 1 *[writes another 1 above the 4]*. 2 times 4 is 8 plus 1 is 9.

$$
\begin{array}{r}
\overset{1}{4}5 \\
\times\,23 \\
\hline
135 \\
90 \\
\hline
103\,5
\end{array}
$$

Task: *848 ÷ 8 =*

Response: 8 goes into 8, 1 time *[writes 1 above 8]*. Subtract 8, get 0. Bring down the 4. 8 goes into 4, 0 times *[writes 0 next to 1]*, 0 times 8 is 0 *[writes 0]*. 4 minus 0 equals 4. Bring down the 8. 48 divided by 8 equals 6 *[writes the 6 next to the 0]*. 106.

```
        106
   8 )848
     - 8
        04
      - 0
        48
      - 48
         0
```

4. Students correctly and meaningfully use an algorithm.

Students correctly and meaningfully use a symbolic algorithm. They provide evidence that they understand underlying properties and place-value concepts. This level of understanding of algorithms occurs in MD Levels 4 and 5. *Note that, for most students, you will not understand if students understand an algorithm unless you ask appropriate questions.*

EXAMPLES

Task: *45 × 23 =*

Response: 3 times 5 is 15, put 5 here *[writes 5]*, carry the 1 up here *[writes 1 above 4]*. 3 times 4 is 12 plus 1 is 13 *[writes 13]*. 2 times 5 is 10, write the 0 *[under 3 in 135]*, carry the 1 *[writes another 1 above the 4]*. 2 times 4 is 8 plus 1 is 9.

```
      1 1
      45
    × 23
    135
    90
   103 5
```

Teacher: Why did you write the 1 above the 4?

Student: Because it's really 1 ten, so you put it in the tens column with the 4 or 40.

Teacher: Why did you write the 13 to the left of 5? Why didn't you just add 13 to 5 *[pointing]*?

Student: Because the 13 is really 130, so the 13 has to go in the tens and hundreds places.

Teacher: Why is the 13 really 130?

Student: Because you're multiplying 3 times 40; the 4 here means 40.

Teacher: Why did you write the 0 from 2 times 5 here *[pointing at the 0]*?

Student: Because it's 20 times 5, which is 1 hundred and 0 tens. That's why I put the little 1 over here, in hundreds.

Teacher: Where does the 90 come from?

Student: It's really 900. It's 20 times 40 equals 8 hundreds, plus the 1 hundred from 20 times 5 makes 9 hundreds.

Task: *848 ÷ 8 =*

Response: 8 goes into 8, 1 time *[writes 1 above 8]*. Subtract 8, get 0. Bring down the 4. 8 goes into 4, 0 times *[writes 0 next to 1]*, 0 times 8 is 0 *[writes 0]*. 4 minus 0 equals 4. Bring down the 8. 48 divided by 8 equals 6 *[writes the 6 next to the 0]*. 106.

$$
\begin{array}{r}
106 \\
8\,\overline{)848} \\
-8 \\
\hline
04 \\
-0 \\
\hline
48 \\
-48 \\
\hline
0
\end{array}
$$

Teacher: Why did you put the 1 above the 8?

Student: Because we are dividing 8 into 8 hundreds, so we put the 1 in the hundreds place.

Teacher: Why did you put the –8 over here?

Student: Because it's 8 hundreds.

Teacher: Why did you subtract 8?

Student: Because we're finding how many 8s are in 848, how many times you can subtract 8 from 848. This 1 up here means that you can subtract 100 eights from 848, and you have 48 left. And there are six 8s in 48. So, you can subtract 106 eights from 848.

Another way students can demonstrate their understanding of a traditional algorithm is to show how it's related to an expanded algorithm, *step by step*, as shown in the discussion for MD Level 5. Or some students can explain an algorithm using place-value blocks.

Using CBA Levels to Develop a Profile of a Student's Reasoning About Multiplication and Division

The CBA assessment tasks are designed to help you assess levels of reasoning, not levels of students. Indeed, a student might use different levels of reasoning on different tasks. For instance, a student might operate at a higher level when using physical materials such as base-ten blocks than when she does not have physical materials to support her thinking. Also, a student might operate at different levels on tasks that are familiar to her or that she has practiced as opposed to tasks that are totally new to her. So, rather than attempting to assign a single level to a student, you should analyze a student's reasoning on several assessment tasks then develop an overall profile of how she is reasoning about the topic.

To develop a CBA profile of a student's reasoning, note which CBA assessment tasks you give to the student, the date, and what CBA level of reasoning the student used on each task. Note whether the student used concrete materials (C), drew pictures (D), used paper-and-pencil to write computations (PP), or did the problem strictly mentally (M). Record whether the student answered the questions correctly or not (C or I). Some teachers also note whether a student was being guided by a teacher (T) or worked on the task without any help (WH). These annotations can be quite important in monitoring student progress. For instance, if in the initial assessment a student uses one level of reasoning with the help of concrete materials but in a subsequent assessment the student uses the same level of reasoning implemented mentally, the student has made considerable progress.

As shown below, a CBA profile provides an excellent picture of student reasoning that can be monitored throughout the school year.

CBA Reasoning Profile

PD, Grade 3, Multiplication and Division

Step 1: *Record What PD Did on CBA Problems*

Single-Digit Problems

For single-digit products, PD consistently derived facts from other facts using a variety of number properties. So, PD consistently used SD Level 3.1 and SD 3.2 reasoning correctly.

1. $8 \times 13 = 104$ What is $9 \times 13 =$ _____?

   PD: *117, because 9 is 1 more than 8, so I add one more 13.*

2. $7 \times 14 = 98$ What is $14 \times 7 =$ _____?

> **PD:** [Almost immediately] *98. It's sort of the same thing; it's just reversed.*

3. I have 20 cubes. I want to put them into containers so there are 5 cubes in each container. How many containers do I need?

> **PD:** *$20 \div 5 = 4$. Division is just multiplication backward; 5 times 4 = 20, so $20 \div 5$ is 4.*

Multidigit Problems

For multidigit products, the picture is less clear. On the one hand, PD is sometimes able to skip-count a group of skip-counts. This is MD Level 2.2.

4. Matt has 120 cubes. He wants to put the cubes into bags, with 15 cubes in each bag. How many bags does he need?

> **PD:** *Four 15s is 60. So, eight 15s is 120. So, 8 would be the answer because I used eight 15s to get 120.*

However, as shown below, when using MD Level 2.2 reasoning, PD exhibited two difficulties. First, several times he made a basic fact error that caused his otherwise correct reasoning to fail.

5. Mary has 84 cookies. She wants to divide them equally among 4 people. How many cookies does each person get?

> **PD:** *Four 4s is 12. Eight 4s is 24; twelve 4s is 36; sixteen 4s is 48; twenty 4s is 60; twenty-four 4s is 72; twenty-eight 4s is 84; so the answer would be 28.*

$$84 \div 4 = 28$$

Second, as the problems get more complex, PD seemed to get lost in his attempts to skip-count a group of skip-counts.

6. $128 \div 16 =$ _____

   PD: *Two 16s is 32* [writes 32]; *eight 16s is 64* [writes 64]; *and twelve 16s is 128* [writes 128], *and that's* [the 128 he wrote] *that right there* [the 128 in the original problem—draws path between them]. *So, the answer would be 12.* [He writes the 12 in the answer space and 4, 8, 12 beside the 32, 64, and 128 he wrote earlier.]

PD is also able to operate on base-ten decompositions on his own for two partial products (MD Level 3.2) and, with some help, for four partial products (MD Level 3.3). But he still makes fact errors and gets lost in more complex problems, so without guidance, he uses MD Level 3.3 incorrectly.

7. $96 \div 4 = 24$ $96 \div 24 =$ _____

   PD: $96 \div 24 = 4$.

   Teacher: *How could you check to see if your answer of 4 is correct?*

   PD: [Writing answers] *four 20s is 80 and four 4s is 16, and 80 + 16 = 96.*

8. To find 32 times 24, Emily reasoned as follows:

   Emily: $30 \times 20 = 600$; $30 \times 4 = 120$; $2 \times 20 = 40$; $2 \times 4 = 8$; $600 + 120 + 40 + 8 = 768$. *So, 768 is the answer.*

   Teacher: *Suppose we had* 25×14. *Could you use Emily's method to solve that?*

   PD: 20×10 *is 20 tens; that would be 200.* $20 \times 4 = 60$. 5×10 *is 50.* 5×4 *equals 20.* $200 + 60 + 50 + 20 = 330$.

In the following problem, PD is unable to correctly implement a four-partial-product strategy.

9. 45 × 34 = _____

> **PD:** *I broke it [the 34] up into 24 and 10 [writes above and below 34]. Twenty 5s is 100, and ten 5s is 150, and another four 5s would be 175. Now 40 × 34. 3 × 4 is 12, so 40 × 30 would be 120; so that's a 0, and I don't need to do anything to it.* [Draws paths from 175 to 120 and adds, getting 295.]

45 × 34 = _____

24
34 × 5 = 175
10

40 + 34

120

295

Step 2: *Construct a CBA Levels Summary Chart for PD*

Task	Level	Correct/ Incorrect	Comment	Mode*
Single-Digit Tasks				
1	SD3.2	C		M
2	SD3.2	C		M
3	SD3.1, 3.2	C		M
Multidigit Tasks				
4	MD2.2	C		M
5	MD2.2	I	Fact error, concept correct	PP
6	MD2.2	I	Concept error	PP
7	MD3.2	C	Guidance given	PP
8	MD3.3	I	Fact error	PP
9	MD3.1	I	Fact error, concept error	PP

* M = mental, PP = pencil and paper

Goal 1. PD needs practice on his basic facts. He tends to make mistakes when he is implementing a more complex computation, suggesting that many of his facts are not yet completely automatic.

Goal 2. PD needs to focus on attaining MD Level 2.3 then MD Level 2.4 before moving on to MD Level 3.

Goal 3. PD needs to work on MD Level 3.1 for multiples of ten.

Goal 4. Once PD has attained mastery of MD Levels 2.3, 2.4, and 3.1, he should review 3.2, then focus strongly on 3.3, then 4.

RECOMMENDATIONS For each goal, have PD do the problem and observe if he uses the type of reasoning targeted by that goal. If he does not, you might demonstrate that type of reasoning for him and see if he makes sense of it. But don't demand that he use it.

For Goal 1, use flash cards.

For Goals 2 and 3, use problems such as the following:

What is 5 × 10? Predict an answer then skip-count to check.

What is 7 × 30? Predict an answer then skip-count to check. And so on.

What is 6 × 47? Predict an answer then skip-count to check. [Can skip-count 6 × 40 first then 6 × 7.] And so on.

For Goal 4, use problems such as the following:

To find 32 times 24, Emily reasoned as follows:

30 × 20 = 600; 30 × 4 = 120; 2 × 20 = 40; 2 × 4 = 8

600 + 120 + 40 + 8 = 768. So, 768 is the answer.

Suppose we had 45 × 23. Could you use Emily's method to solve that?

Chapter 3

Instructional Strategies for Single-Digit Multiplication and Division

Once you have used the assessment tasks to determine which levels of reasoning students are using, you can use the teaching suggestions and instructional tasks described in this chapter to tailor instruction to precisely fit students' learning needs. For each major level of reasoning, there are suggestions for teaching that encourage and support students' movement to the next important type of reasoning in the sequence.

For students to make progress, have them do several problems of a specific type until you see them move to the next level or you become convinced that they are not quite ready to move on to the next level. In the latter case, try a different kind of problem suggested for that level.

Note that attaining higher levels of reasoning about multiplication and division, especially the highest levels, is interrelated with attaining higher levels of reasoning about place value and the properties of numbers (see *Cognition-Based Assessment and Teaching of Place Value* for a detailed description of students' development of place-value reasoning). Also, students' level of reasoning for division will generally lag behind their level for multiplication. However, after a student progresses a step in level of sophistication for multiplication, you can, depending on the level, try to get the student to move to the same level for division.

Students should develop a great deal of proficiency with single-digit multiplication and division before progressing to multidigit multiplication and division.

Teaching Students at SD Level 0: Constructing Initial Meaning for Multiplication and Division

Give students problems that involve multiplication and division in physical situations (e.g., enumerating the total number of objects in a set of equivalent groups). Placing equal sets of objects in physical containers can help students understand that groups, not just individual objects, are countable.

Hand out **STUDENT SHEET 1** and read through the problems with the students. (All of the student sheets referenced in Chapter 3 and Chapter 4 can be found at www.heinemann.com/products/E04344.aspx. (Click on the "Companion Resources" tab.)) Then give each student (or group of students) twenty cubes and six cups they can use to help them solve the problems.

At first, you may have to ask guiding questions to help students understand the physical situations. For example, suppose students are working on this problem:

George has 4 cups. There are 2 cubes in each cup. How many cubes does George have altogether?

For students having difficulty with this problem, ask the following questions to help them physically represent the situation the problem describes.

- How many cups does George have? Okay, put 4 cups in front of you.
- How many cubes are in each cup? Put 2 cubes in each cup.
- How many cubes are there altogether? Can you count all the cubes in the cups? Do you need to dump the cubes out of the cups so that you can count them?

Once students understand situations about cubes and cups, give problems that are not about cubes and cups but can be acted out with cubes. (See Problems 3, 6, and 7, for example.)

You may have to provide similar guidance for division problems. For example, suppose students are working on this problem:

Zach has 12 cubes and 3 cups. He puts the same number of cubes into each cup. How many cubes are in each cup?

For students having difficulty with this problem, ask the following questions to help them physically represent the situation the problem describes.

- How many cups does Zach have? Okay, put 3 cups in front of you.
- How can we put the cubes into the cups so that each cup has the same number of cubes in it? Deal the cubes to the cups one at a time like you deal cards.
- *[When all the cubes are dealt]* How many cubes are in each cup? Count them. Are there the same number of cubes in each cup?

Teaching Students at SD Level 1: Increasing the Sophistication of Counting by Ones

Teaching Students at Level SD Level 1.1: Moving to Counting Imagined Objects or Counting Words

Counting Imagined Objects

To help students progress beyond using physical objects, it is quite helpful to have them explicitly try to imagine or visualize physical situations. Hand out **STUDENT SHEET 2** . Read the first problem aloud, but do not provide cubes or cups. Ask students if they can solve the problem by picturing the cups and cubes in their minds. (Give students enough time so that they can solve the problem by themselves.) If they can't solve the problem by imagining it, suggest that they draw a picture that will help them solve it. If they cannot solve the problem by drawing a picture (or if they get incorrect answers), give them cubes and cups. After they have used the cups and cubes, ask them to close their eyes and do the problem again, but in their minds.

Have the students do the remaining problems in the same way as described above. (Working through the problems one at a time provides more opportunities to see how students are thinking and to provide *guided* practice to students.) The first problem may be easier to complete than the second two because multiplication is generally easier for students than division. If students struggle with the first problem, have them solve another simple multiplication problem involving cups and cubes before moving on to the division problems.

Having students gain facility working with *imagined* groups of objects is an excellent way for them to progress to counting count words.

Counting Count Words

Using problems like those on **STUDENT SHEETS 1** and **2** , read the first problem aloud but do not provide cubes or cups. Ask students if they can solve the problem without using cubes or pictures. If students cannot solve the problem, suggest they count. If they still can't solve it, suggest they use their fingers. If they still can't solve it, you or another student might demonstrate the counting count words strategy. For example,

There are 4 cups and 2 cubes in each cup. How many cubes are there altogether?

> *[Demonstrate the actions as you describe them to students.]* Mary solved this problem by saying, "1, 2" as she put up one finger; "3, 4" as she put up a second finger; "5, 6" as she put up a third finger; and "7, 8" as she put up a fourth finger. She said, "There are 8 cubes." Is Mary's way of doing this problem right? Why? Why did Mary put up 4 fingers? *[Students say, There are 4 cups.]* Why did Mary count two times for each finger? *[Students say, There are 2 cubes in each cup.]*

Another way to help students progress to counting count words is to have them write the count words while using their fingers to represent groups. So, for the first problem on Student Sheet 2, students write "1, 2" as they raise their first finger, "3, 4" as they raise their second finger, "5, 6" as they raise their third finger, and "7, 8" as they raise their fourth finger.

Do the remaining problems the same way as described above.

Moving from Counting by Ones (Level 1) to Skip-Counting (Level 2)

Our next goal is for students to progress to iteration by skip-counting. As we try to help students learn to skip-count to solve multiplication and division problems, almost all of them will do it in stages, moving through various combinations of skip-counting, counting by ones, repeated addition and subtraction, and skip-counting by parts.

Even though there are four levels of sophistication in skip-counting, only two serve as major instructional goals—Levels 2.1 and 2.3. However, no matter how you teach these two goals, some students will use Levels 2.2 and 2.4 reasoning,

Teaching Students at Levels 1.2 or 1.3: Beginning Skip-Counting

Give students the same type of problems as on Student Sheets 1 and 2 (see **STUDENT SHEET 3**) . But now, ask students if they can solve the problems without counting all the numbers by ones. Students might use repeated addition or subtraction or skip-counting, or a combination, on these problems.

Start with problems that require skip-counting by 2s and 5s because these numbers are the easiest to skip-count.

As students begin learning skip-count sequences, they often know the first several multiples in the sequence but have to figure out later ones. For example, in skip-counting by 3s, a student might know 3, 6, 9 but not know what number comes next. Some students will determine the next multiple (12) by counting by ones (3, 6, 9; 10, 11, *12*); others will add, 9 + 3 = 12. Ask students who do not spontaneously use addition or counting by ones to continue an unknown skip-count sequence if counting by ones or adding will help them. Also, students may progress to skip-counting in some contexts (with concrete materials) before other contexts (drawing or using counting words).

Teaching Students at Levels 1.3, 2.1, or 2.2: Progressing to Fluent Skip-Counting (Level 2.3)

At first, help students link verbal skip-counts with visual iterations of the sets. For example, when counting by 2s, the class might say *two* while you put two objects onto the overhead projector screen, *four* while you put two more objects onto the screen, and so on.

It is also helpful to use multiples arrays. The array below is for helping students to count by 4s:

Problem: [On an overhead, show an array of squares like the 4-by-6 unlabeled array on the left below.] *I put these* squares *in rows of 4* [point to rows]. *I want to know how many* squares *there are altogether. Let's count all the squares in the rows by ones* [write numerals as students count squares by ones as shown].

1	2	3	4
5	6	7	8
9	10	11	12
13	14	15	16
17	18	19	20
21	22	23	24

Is there any way we could have figured out how many squares *there are without counting every single* square? *Could we count in a different way?*

To help students, you can ask the following kinds of questions:

How many squares *are there in the first row?*

How many squares *are there in the first two rows? How do you know?*

How many squares *are there in the first three rows? How do you know?*

Try to get students to see that the numbers in the right-hand column tell the total number of squares in successive sets of rows. For example, the 8 tells how many squares are in the first two rows.

Which numbers tell us how to count the squares by 4s? Why?

How do we count the squares by 4s?

Have students work on **CBA STUDENT SHEET 4** 🔽 , in which they skip-count then check their answers by counting by ones.

When skip-counting by tens, you can have students look at a hundreds chart. The shaded squares in the chart illustrate counting by tens.

1	2	3	4	5	6	7	8	9	10
11	12	13	14	15	16	17	18	19	20
21	22	23	24	25	26	27	28	29	30
31	32	33	34	35	36	37	38	39	40
41	42	43	44	45	46	47	48	49	50
51	52	53	54	55	56	57	58	59	60
61	62	63	64	65	66	67	68	69	70
71	72	73	74	75	76	77	78	79	80
81	82	83	84	85	86	87	88	89	90
91	92	93	94	95	96	97	98	99	100

Once students understand skip-counting, give problems in which the objects to be skip-counted are not visible. See the gum problems on **STUDENT SHEET 5** 🔽 .

If students do not skip-count on the gum problems, ask questions that suggest it: *"How can counting by 2s help you solve this problem?"*

If students have difficulty solving the gum problems, provide supporting visual materials. For instance, for Problem 1, show the picture below and ask the question again.

Each pack of gum has 2 pieces of gum in it. How many pieces of gum are in 4 packs of gum?

If students can't use skip-counting, use pictures to illustrate the connection between counting the number of packs and skip-counting the number of pieces.

[Show the picture below] There are 2 sticks of gum in each pack. Let's count them like this: 1 pack is 2 sticks, 2 packs is 4 sticks, 3 packs is 6 sticks, 4 packs is 8 sticks. How can counting by 2s help us solve this problem?

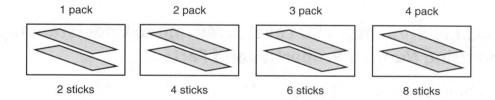

As practice, you can have the class recite verbal skip-count sequences:

- ▦ Can you skip-count by 2s? Show me.
- ▦ Can you skip-count by 5s? Show me.
- ▦ Can you skip-count by 10s? Show me.
- ▦ Can you skip-count by 3s? Show me.
- ▦ Can you skip-count by 4s? Show me.

Once students have developed fluency skip-counting to solve multiplication problems, help them extend this procedure to division problems (see **STUDENT SHEET 6**).

Teaching Students at SD Levels 2.3 and 2.4: Moving to Using Number Facts

When students solve multiplication and division problems using the reasoning described in Levels 1 and 2, they are meaningfully solving these problems because the problems either (1) focus on physical contexts that make sense to students or (2) build on already understood mathematical procedures (such as counting or adding). If students do enough of these problems, they will naturally start remembering some problem answers. For instance, if they have done several problems involving 4 groups of 2 using physical manipulation or skip-counting, many students will remember that the answer is 8.

Introducing multiplication and division notation and language to describe these problems and their answers can help students consolidate and recall these "basic facts." For instance, help students who have developed fluency in skip-counting to consolidate their answers into known facts as follows.

- ▦ If I have 4 cups with 2 cubes in each cup, how many cubes do I have? (Students might have to solve this problem using skip-counting or even using cubes.)
- ▦ If I have 4 packs of gum with 2 pieces in each pack, how many pieces of gum do I have?
- ▦ If there are 4 groups of students and 2 students in each group, how many students are there?
- ▦ So, 4 groups of 2 things is what?

- What is *4 times 2*?
- We write 4 times 2 equals 8 as $4 \times 2 = 8$. This means that 4 groups of 2 things is 8 things altogether.

Teaching Students at SD Level 3: Moving to Understanding and Using Number Properties and Facts

Teaching Students at Level 3.1: Moving to Using Number Properties to Derive Facts

Once students know some multiplication and division facts, they can begin using number *properties* to derive answers to related problems. They discover these properties by looking for patterns as they solve carefully chosen problem sequences or by looking carefully at physical or pictorial representations.

Although the algebraic forms for these properties are shown for the sake of completeness, elementary school students generally learn these properties intuitively or based on pictorial representations. At this age, learning the algebraic representations is not nearly as important as acquiring an intuitive, conceptual understanding of these ideas.

Commutative Property

Algebraic Form: $a \times b = b \times a$

Verbal Description: When multiplying two numbers, it does not matter which number comes first.

Have students compute answers to pairs of multiplication problems with the order of factors reversed. Ask them what pattern they detect after solving several pairs of problems.

What's 5 × 3?   *What's 3 × 5?*

What's 7 × 5?   *What's 5 × 7? (etc.)*

You might have to rephrase some of these problems in terms of physical representations. For instance, you might ask students, "What is 5 times 3? *How many candies do I have altogether if I have 5 bags with 3 candies in each bag?*" "What is 3 times 5? *How many candies do I have altogether if I have 3 bags with 5 candies in each bag?*"

You can also have students use a calculator to compute pairs of problems that illustrate the commutative property. Students should record all the problem statements and their answers and look for patterns.

$5 \times 3 =$ _____ $3 \times 5 =$ _____

$8 \times 6 =$ _____ $6 \times 8 =$ _____

A calculator can also be used to show that the commutative property *is not true for division*:

$12 \div 6 =$ _____ $6 \div 12 =$ _____

$20 \div 4 =$ _____ $4 \div 20 =$ _____

To help students understand *why* the commutative property for multiplication is true, you can use arrays, giving each factor a specific meaning. For instance, if we interpret 5×3 as 5 groups of 3, we can picture 5×3 as shown below:

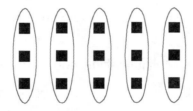

So, for this array, we can ask students: If I have 5 groups of 3 squares, how many squares do I have?

But this array of squares can also be viewed as 3 groups of 5, which is 3×5.

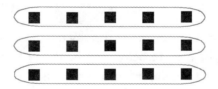

So, we can ask students: If I have 3 groups of 5 squares, how many squares do I have?

Because 5 groups of 3 can be rearranged as 3 groups of 5, 5 times 3 equals 3 times 5.

Repeat this line of questioning with other arrays, such as 3 by 6, 4 by 5, and so on.

Associative Property

Algebraic Form: $a \times (b \times c) = (a \times b) \times c$

Verbal Description: *When multiplying three numbers in order, it does not matter which pair of numbers you multiply first.*

One way of using the associative property is to change a problem into an alternate problem. For example, consider the problem 4×9. Because $4 = 2 \times 2$, we can think of 4×9 as $(2 \times 2) \times 9$. But by the associative property,

$$(2 \times 2) \times 9 = 2 \times (2 \times 9) = 2 \times (18)$$

Mentally, students might implement this reasoning quickly and intuitively, saying:

$$4 \times 9 = 2 \times 18 = 20 + 16 = 36$$

So, this student uses the known fact that $2 \times 18 = 36$ to solve the problem 4×9.

Inverse Relation Between Multiplication and Division

Algebraic Form: $a \div b = c$ *if and only if* $b \times c = a$

Help students discover the important relationship between multiplication and division by detecting patterns in sets of problems.

What is 5 × 3?   What is 3 × 5?   What is 15 ÷ 3?   What is 15 ÷ 5?

Help students see why this relationship is true by decomposing arrays into equal subgroups. For instance, the picture below can be used to answer the question, *What is 5 groups of 3 (5 × 3 = 15)?* The picture also can be used to answer the question, *If 15 is divided into 5 equal groups, how many are in each group (15 ÷ 5 = 3)?* Or *How many groups of 3 are in 15 (15 ÷ 3 = 5)?*

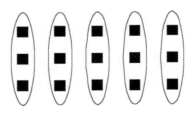

Distributive Property

Understanding the distributive property is critical to multiplying and dividing, especially when the operations involve multidigit numbers.

Distributive Property of Multiplication	Application to Deriving Answers
$a \times (b + c) = (a \times b) + (a \times c)$	$7 \times (4 + 2) = (7 \times 4) + (7 \times 2) = 28 + 14$
Distributive Property of Division $(a + b) \div c = (a \div c) + (b \div c)$	$45 \div 5 = (20 + 25) \div 5 =$ $(20 \div 5) + (25 \div 5) =$ $4 + 5 = 9$

You can illustrate the distributive property with grouping diagrams like that shown below. Eight groups of 7 equals 8 groups of 3 plus 8 groups of 4.

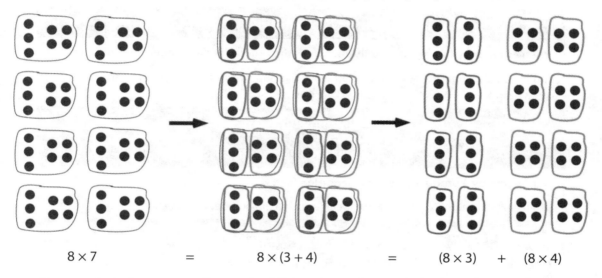

$$8 \times 7 \qquad = \qquad 8 \times (3 + 4) \qquad = \qquad (8 \times 3) \quad + \quad (8 \times 4)$$

Once students know some facts, ask additional questions to help them derive related facts using the distributive property. For example,

For 6 × 3, ask, *What is 5 × 3, 5 groups of 3?* [15] *What is one more 3?* [18]

For 7 × 8, ask, *What is 5 × 8, 5 groups of 8?* [40] *What is two more 8s, two more groups of 8?* [40 + 16]

Other Properties

Other important properties and special thinking strategies are listed in the table below.

These properties can be discovered by asking sequences of questions that highlight the property or by discussing the justifications listed in the table. For instance, for the "1 property" you can ask: *What is 5 times 1? What is 5 groups with 1 cube in each group?* Or *What is 1 group with 5 objects in it?*

For 2 × 8, ask, *What is 8 + 8 [doubles]?*

Multiply by 0 Property
Any number times 0 equals 0.
Intuitive Justification: 5 × 0 can be interpreted as 5 groups with no objects in them or as no groups with 5 objects in them.
Multiply by 1 Property (1 is the multiplicative identity)
When any number, except 0, is multiplied by 1, the product is the original number.
Intuitive Justification: 5 × 1 can be interpreted as 5 groups with 1 object in each group—so count from 1 to 5—or as 1 group with 5 objects in it.
Special Thinking Strategies
Doubles (multiplying by 2)
Multiplying by 2 produces a doubles addition fact.
Intuitive Justification: Two times a number is equal to the number plus itself: 2 × 3 = 3 + 3
Threes
Three times a number is double the number plus the number.
Intuitive Justification: 3 × 5 = 10 + 5.
Fives
Five times a number equals half of ten times the number.
Intuitive Justification: 5 × 8 = 80 ÷ 2.
Nines
Nine times a number equals ten times the number minus the number.
Intuitive Justification: 9 × 7 = (10 × 7) − 7 = 70 − 7

Cognition-Based Assessment and Teaching of Multiplication and Division

×	0	1	2	3	4	5	6	7	8	9	Property or Strategy
0	0	0	0	0	0	0	0	0	0	0	Multiply by 0
1	0	1	2	3	4	5	6	7	8	9	Multiply by 1
2	0	2	4	6	8	10	12	14	16	18	Doubles
3	0	3	6	9	12	15	18	21	24	27	Threes
4	0	4	8	12	16	20	24	28	32	36	
5	0	5	10	15	20	25	30	35	40	45	Fives
6	0	6	12	18	24	30	36	42	48	54	
7	0	7	14	21	28	35	42	49	56	63	
8	0	8	16	24	32	40	48	56	64	72	
9	0	9	18	27	36	45	54	63	72	81	Nines

Practicing Basic Facts

When you are sure that students understand the meaning of multiplication and division and they have started to remember many of the facts, it is important for students' mathematical fluency to help them practice these facts. Once students are fluent with most multiplication facts, have them practice division facts (or start mixing in division problems with multiplication problems).

Flash Cards

One of the best ways of having students practice their facts is using flash cards (cards with problems on the front and answers on the back). Each student should have his or her own set of 100 cards.

Have a parent or another student present a student a set of 10 cards, one card at a time. The student who is presented with the card has about three seconds to say the answer out loud. The idea is for students to either recall the fact or derive it very quickly (often you cannot tell which students are doing). If the student gets the answer correct, say "correct" and put the card in one pile. If the student gives an incorrect answer, say "incorrect" and put it in another pile. After all ten cards are used, have students figure out the answers to the cards for which their answers were incorrect, reciting the problem and its answer after each problem is solved. After the student has figured out the correct answers to incorrect problems, reshuffle the cards and present them again. Keep going until all the cards are answered correctly. In general, choose sets of ten cards in which the student does not know about three of the answers. If the student misses more than three problems, before proceeding, delete cards from the incorrect set so that only three remain. Keep changing the sets of ten cards (again, with at most three cards presenting unknown facts). Once students are fluent with sets of ten facts, start increasing the number of cards in the set, perhaps going up to twenty cards at a time. Change sets frequently as students become successful.

Games

Another way to help students build fluency with multiplication and division facts is the use of games. For instance, pairs of students can play multiplication flash card "war," like the classic card game. Each student is dealt 25 multiplication flash cards, which are then stacked in front of the players "missing answer" side up. In the first turn, players put their top cards in the middle, each saying the product as they play their card. The player who has the larger product wins both cards. Students can check their product answers by flipping over the cards. Students can also play the same game with division cards.

Timed Tests?

I recommend that you *not* use timed tests in trying to produce student fluency with multiplication and division facts. Although timed tests can indicate to you which students know all their facts, such tests are not very good at determining which facts students know. And as described above, knowing which facts students know and don't know is critical in organizing their practice on the facts. Timed tests also produce much anxiety in students who have difficulty memorizing the facts, making their learning of facts even more difficult.

Chapter 4

Instructional Strategies for Multidigit Multiplication and Division

$$\times \div$$

Once you have used CBA Multiplication and Division assessment tasks to determine which CBA levels of reasoning students are using, you can use the teaching suggestions and instructional tasks described in this chapter to tailor instruction to precisely fit students' learning needs. Again, note that attaining the highest levels of reasoning about multiplication and division depends on attaining higher levels of reasoning about place value and the properties of numbers.

Keep in mind that students are not ready for multidigit problems in multiplication and division until they have reached SD Level 3 for single-digit problems. Also, give students who are reasoning at MD Level 1 (Counting by Ones) or MD Level 2 (Skip-Counting) only problems in which one of the factors has two digits. Solving problems with two multidigit factors is too tedious at these levels.

Once you have identified a student's predominant level of reasoning, you need to provide the student with an appropriate opportunity to progress to the next higher level of reasoning. To do this, have the student do enough problems of a specific type suggested for his or her level until you see him or her progress to the next CBA level. If you become convinced that the student cannot move to the next level on this type of problem, try a different type of problem suggested for that level. If the student still cannot move forward, try some instructional activities suggested for the previous level of reasoning. Another instructional strategy is to ask more directive questions or give suggestions that lead the student to move to the next level of reasoning.

However, if you are more directive, be sure to give additional problems without such direction to see if the student can use the higher level reasoning without your help.

Relating Multiplication and Division

Students' level of reasoning for division will generally lag behind their level for multiplication. After a student progresses one major level for multiplication (e.g., from Level 1 to Level 2), your next goal might be to get the student to move to the same major level for division. You can continue this back and forth between multiplication and division for Levels 1–4. However, once students reach Level 4 (Expanded Algorithms) for multiplication, if your curriculum includes traditional algorithms, encourage them to move to Level 5 (*Understanding* Traditional Algorithms) for multiplication then have them progress through Levels 4 and 5 for division.

Teaching Students at MD Level 1: Helping Students Skip-Count Multidigit Numbers

The goal for students who are reasoning at MD Level 1 is to extend their skip-counting capability from single-digit to multidigit numbers. We want to help students move from Level MD1 to Levels MD2.1 and MD2.3. As students move forward, they face two different problem situations. In Situation 1, students need to skip-count single-digit numbers a multidigit number of times (for example, skip-counting by five 12 times to find 5×12). This situation is a straightforward extension of Levels SD2.1 and SD2.3 reasoning. In Situation 2, students skip-count multidigit numbers a single-digit number of times (for example, skip-counting by 12 five times to find 12×5), which is considerably more difficult. Once students are regularly skip-counting single digit numbers for Situation 1 problems, we shift our focus to Situation 2 problems—developing facility with skip-counting multidigit numbers.

Note that although MD Level 1.3 reasoning is never a goal of instruction, this type of reasoning occurs for many students as they progress through the sublevels of MD Level 1. Also, recall from the discussion of the inverse relationship between multiplication and division given in Chapter 1 that we can replace division computations with related multiplication computations, which are generally easier for students to implement. Thus, the major focus throughout Levels MD1 and MD2 remains on multiplication rather than division.

Teaching Students at MD Level 1.1: Encouraging Multidigit Skip-Counting of Physical/Visual Objects

CBA instruction should focus on Situation 1. However, students may encounter Situation 2 problems outside CBA instruction, so you must also be prepared to handle Situation 2.

Situation 1

The number of groups has two digits and the number of objects in each group has one digit. For example, suppose students draw 12 sets of 5 dots to solve the problem: *A bag contains 5 gumballs. Emily has 12 bags. How many gumballs does Emily have altogether?* After students count "gumballs" by ones, encourage them to skip-count gumballs by fives by asking: *Is there a faster way to count? Can you count by fives?* To support this reasoning, you might even draw circles around sets of 5 dots.

To encourage Level 1.2 reasoning, after students finish skip-counting physical objects, have them try skip-counting again but have them *write* the skip-count numbers.

Situation 2

The number of groups has one digit and the number of objects in each group has two digits. For example, *A carton contains 12 eggs. Emily has 5 cartons. How many eggs does Emily have altogether?* If a student makes 5 groups of 12 cubes then counts all the cubes by ones, ask the student if she can use place-value blocks to do the problem. This should encourage at least Level 1.4 reasoning.

Teaching Students at MD Levels 1.2 and 1.3: Encouraging Verbal Multidigit Skip-Counting

As above, the two problem situations should be treated differently with instruction focusing on Situation 1 problems.

Situation 1

The number of groups has two digits and the number of objects in each group has one digit. For example, *A bag contains 5 gumballs. Emily has 12 bags. How many gumballs does Emily have altogether?* Suppose a student counts by ones: 1, 2, 3, 4, 5 *[puts up one finger]*; 6, 7, 8, 9, 10 *[puts up another finger]*; … 46, 47, 48, 49, 50 *[puts up a tenth finger then puts all 10 fingers down]*; … 56, 57, 58, 59, 60 *[puts up a twelfth finger]*. Encourage the student to skip-count by fives by asking: *Is there a faster way to count? Can you count by fives?*

To progress, students need to extend their skip-counting of single-digit numbers beyond 10 iterations. **STUDENT SHEETS 7** and **8** give problems that encourage students to do this. Student Sheet 7 reminds students of the meaning of skip-counting and helps them extend it beyond 10 skip-counts. Introduce the problems by covering all but the first row of the array and asking: *How many rectangles are there in this row?* Then uncover the next row and ask: *How many rectangles are there altogether in these two rows?* Continue this line of questioning for several successive rows. Ask students, *How do we know which numbers come next in the right-hand column?* Be sure that students see the different ways that successive numbers in the right-hand column can be generated: counting by ones, adding 5, skip-counting by 5.

Student Sheet 8 gives students further practice with skip-counting beyond 10 counts but with only partial pictorial support. If students have difficulty, show them pictures with the correct number of packs of gum. For instance, for Problem 1 (12 × 2), show them a picture of 12 packs of gum with two sticks in each.

Situation 2

The number of groups has one digit and the number of objects in each group has two digits. For example, *A carton contains 12 eggs. Emily has 5 cartons. How many eggs does Emily have altogether?* A student may count by ones: 1, 2, 3 … 11, 12 *[puts up one finger]*; 13, 14 … 23, 24 *[puts up another finger]*; … 48, 49 … 59, 60 *[puts up a sixth finger]*. Ask this student if there is a faster way to count. If the student responds that counting by twelves would be faster, suggest using place-value blocks to do this, which should encourage at least Level 1.4 reasoning.

Teaching Students at MD Level 1.4: Moving To Iterating Multidigit Numbers with Repeated Addition and Subtraction

For students to progress beyond MD Level 1.4 for Situation 2 problems, they must be able to find the values of multidigit numbers by counting tens and ones (this is CBA Place-Value Level 2). You can help these students progress to MD Level 2 reasoning through the following three-step process.

Step 1: Reflecting on Skip-Counting a Multidigit Number

Have students represent, for example, 3 × 26 as 3 sets of 2 ten-blocks and 6 one-blocks. Students at CBA Place-Value Level 2 or above will group the ten-blocks together and the one-blocks together and say *[pointing at the 6 ten-blocks]* 60; *[pointing at the one-blocks]* 61, 62, 63 … 78.

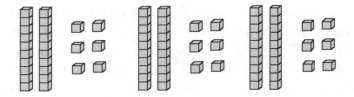

Cognition-Based Assessment and Teaching of Multiplication and Division

You can ask: *Use the place-value blocks to skip-count 26 three times. Write each skip-count number.* If students have difficulty, you can demonstrate:

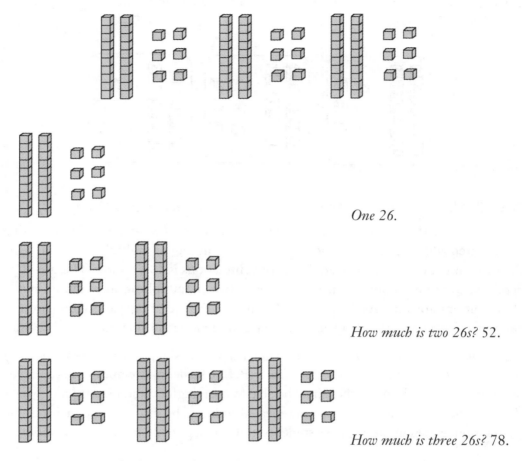

One 26.

How much is two 26s? 52.

How much is three 26s? 78.

To recognize 78 in the last picture, students might say: 6 ten-blocks makes 60, 10 one-blocks makes it 70, and 8 more one-blocks makes 78.

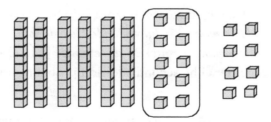

You can also relate these pictures to division. For instance, the picture below shows that 3 groups of 26 is 78, so 78 ÷ 3 which can be interpreted as 78 divided into three equal groups which gives 26 in each group, and 78 ÷ 26 can be interpreted as how many 26s in 78 which is 3.

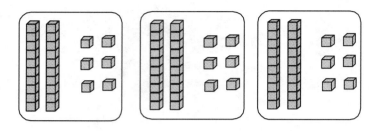

Step 2: Moving Students to Repeated Addition and Subtraction

As you work with students in Step 2, keep in mind that the strategy of skip-counting by repeated addition or subtraction is feasible for multidigit multiplication and division only if the number of additions or subtractions is 10 or fewer. The use of repeated addition reinforces the connection between multiplication, addition, and skip-counting forward. As described in Chapter 1, the use of repeated subtraction reinforces the connection between division, subtraction, and skip-counting backward.

MULTIPLICATION AS REPEATED ADDITION   Begin Step 2 by asking, *How can we use addition to solve 3 × 26 without using place-value blocks?* (Before students attempt to use repeated addition for multiplication, they must be able to meaningfully and fluently add two-digit numbers.) As students engage in repeated addition, be sure to relate their results to iteration. For example, suppose students find 3 groups of 26 by repeated addition:

$$\begin{array}{r} 26 \\ + 26 \\ \hline 52 \end{array} \qquad \begin{array}{r} 52 \\ + 26 \\ \hline 78 \end{array}$$

   Help students explicitly recognize the relationship between repeated addition and iteration by asking: *How many 26s did you add? How do you know? Can you use your addition problems to skip-count (iterate) 26 three times?* [The first addition problem shows two 26s added together. The second addition problem shows the result of adding a third 26.]

DIVISION AS REPEATED SUBTRACTION   Once students understand using repeated addition to solve multidigit multiplication problems, you can have them use repeated subtraction to solve multidigit division problems. (Students must already be proficient with multidigit subtraction, including problems involving regrouping.) For example, for 80 ÷ 16, students can do the following sequence of repeated subtractions:

$$\begin{array}{r} 80 \\ - 16 \\ \hline 64 \end{array} \qquad \begin{array}{r} 64 \\ - 16 \\ \hline 48 \end{array} \qquad \begin{array}{r} 48 \\ - 16 \\ \hline 32 \end{array} \qquad \begin{array}{r} 32 \\ - 16 \\ \hline 16 \end{array} \qquad \begin{array}{r} 16 \\ - 16 \\ \hline 0 \end{array}$$

Again, ask students questions to ensure that they see how this sequence of repeated subtractions shows that $80 \div 16 = 5$. They can observe from the sequence that if you subtract 16 from 80 five times, you get 0, which means that there are five 16s in 80. Of course, they can also relate this division problem to the related sequence of five repeated additions of 16 to get 80.

16	32	48	64
+ 16	+ 16	+ 16	+ 16
32	48	64	80

Step 3: Solidifying Level 2.1

Encourage students to solve a number of multiplication problems by repeated addition. Keep the number of repeated additions small.

Once students develop proficiency using repeated addition for multiplication, give division problems. It is acceptable at first for students to use either repeated addition *or* subtraction for division problems, but be sure that students eventually understand how to use repeated subtraction for division. This knowledge is the foundation for understanding division algorithms.

SAMPLE PROBLEMS

Ask students to use repeated addition to solve the following Situation 2 problems in which a two-digit number is added a single-digit number of times.

$3 \times 18,$ $\qquad 4 \times 35,$ $\qquad 6 \times 23,$ $\qquad 3 \times 47,$ $\qquad$ and so on

Ask students to use repeated subtraction to solve the following Situation 2 problems in which a two-digit number is subtracted a single-digit number of times.

$60 \div 12,$ $\qquad 72 \div 24,$ $\qquad 105 \div 15,$ $\qquad$ and so on

Teaching Students at MD Level 2: Deepening Students' Understanding and Use of Multidigit Skip-Counting

Teaching Students at MD Levels 2.1 and 2.2: Moving to Understanding and Using Skip-Counting of Multidigit Numbers

Our goal for students who are using repeated addition/subtraction at Level 2.1 is to help them move to skip-counting all in Levels 2.3 and skip-counting by place-value parts in 2.4.

On the way to Levels 2.3 and 2.4, some students may use Level 2.2 reasoning, which can be useful in special circumstances. For instance, consider the problem, *What is 12 groups of 25?* Some students will solve this problem by reasoning that *4 groups of 25 is 100; 4 more groups makes 200, and 4 more groups, which is 12 groups altogether, makes 300.* However, because Level 2.2 reasoning is useful only for special problems and because it is difficult for many students to keep track of the number of groups, accept and value this strategy when students spontaneously use it, but do not encourage it.

Moving from Level 2.1 to Level 2.3: Skip-Counting All Multidigit Numbers

Although many students will be able to skip-count some multidigit numbers, the goal should not be "mastery" of skip-counting for all multidigit numbers. Instead, our goal is to help students clearly *understand* the process of skip-counting multidigit numbers.

One activity that is useful for students at this level is completing skip-count tables. See **STUDENT SHEET 9** ⬇ , which gives students problems in which they iterate "easy" multidigit numbers.

Introduce Student Sheet 9 by completing the following two skip-count tables as a class. *We want to complete this skip-count table to find 9 × 10. Try to skip count 10 nine times mentally. If you don't know the next skip-count number, use addition to find it.*

Skip-Count Table for 9 × 10

Number of Groups	1	2	3	4	5	6	7	8	9
Total in Groups	10	20	30	40	50	60	70	80	90

Now let's complete the skip-count table for 5 × 11.

Skip-Count Table for 5 × 11

Number of Groups	1	2	3	4	5				
Total in Groups	11	22	33	44	55				

Once students develop some proficiency with skip-count tables to solve multiplication problems, have them use the same tables to solve division problems. For instance, while looking at the completed skip-count table for 5 × 11, ask, *How can we use this table to figure out 55 ÷ 11? Explain your answer.* [The table shows that 55 is 5 groups of 11, so 55 ÷ 11 = 5.] *How about 44 ÷ 11?*

Teaching Students at MD Level 2.3: Moving to Skip-Counting by Place-Value Parts

Skip-counting multidigit numbers by place-value parts, mentally or using paper and pencil, is not only a reasonable strategy for simple problems, but it is also an important stepping-stone for understanding the powerful reasoning of MD Level 3.

Skip-Counting Multiples of Ten and One Hundred

A critical step toward this strategy is skip-counting multiples of ten. The chart below is one way to help students connect skip-counting by 3s, skip-counting by 30s, and skip-counting by 300s. Some students will need to count by tens to make sense of skip-counting by 30s and hundreds to make sense of skip-counting by 300s.

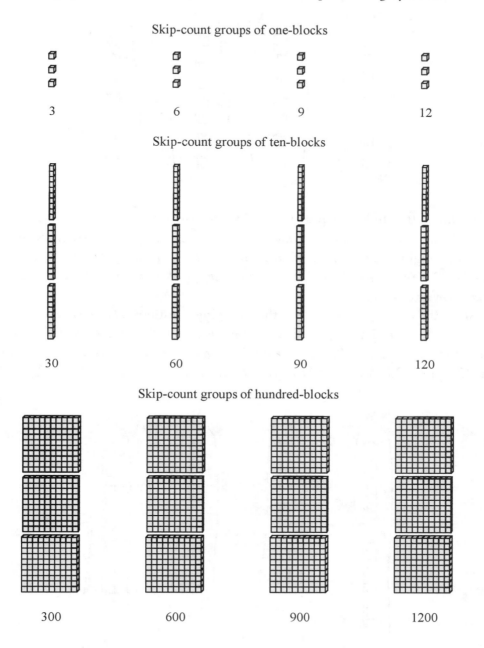

Skip-count groups of one-blocks

| 3 | 6 | 9 | 12 |

Skip-count groups of ten-blocks

| 30 | 60 | 90 | 120 |

Skip-count groups of hundred-blocks

| 300 | 600 | 900 | 1200 |

Skip-Counting Place-Value Parts Using Place-Value Blocks or Pictures

You can use place-value blocks, or pictorial representations of them, to introduce skip-counting multidigit numbers by their place-value parts. Have the student examine the picture representation below, asking, *What is 4 × 13?*

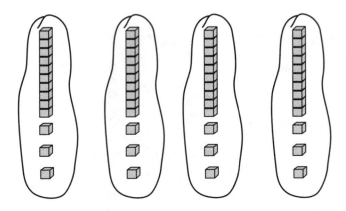

It's fine if the student skip-counts by 13s, but ask if there is another way to do the problem. *Can we use skip-counting by 10s and 3s separately to solve this problem? How?* You might also ask, *One student did this problem by counting 10, 20, 30, 40. 3, 6, 9, 12. 40 + 12 = 52. Do you think this way of doing the problem is correct? Use the picture to explain why or why not.*

Show the picture below and ask the following questions: *How much is 4 groups of 2 tens, or 4 groups of 20?* [Expected response: 20, 40, 60, 80.] *How much is 4 groups of 3?* [Expected response: 3, 6, 9, 12.] *How much is 4 groups of 23?* [Expected response: 80 plus 12 equals 92.] *How do you know your answer is correct?*

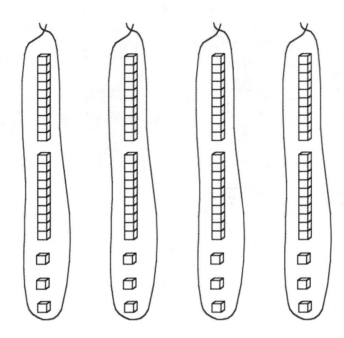

You can use the same pictures to pose the related division problems. For the first picture, ask, *What is 52 ÷ 13? How do you know?* [Four groups of 10 is 10, 20, 30, 40. Four groups of 3 is 3, 6, 9, 12. So, four groups of 13 is 40 + 12 = 52. So, 52 ÷ 13 = 4.] The picture also illustrates 52 ÷ 4. [40 ÷ 4 is 10; 4 tens divided into 4 equal groups is 1 ten in each group. 12 divided into 4 equal groups is 3 in each group. So, 52 divided into 4 equal groups is 1 ten and 3 ones or 13 in each group.] For the second picture, ask, *What is 92 ÷ 13?* Or *What is 92 ÷ 4?*

Skip-Counting Place-Value Parts Using Skip-Count Tables

The table below decomposes skip-counting by 47 into skip-counting by 40 and 7. The last row lists the skip-counts of 47. Each entry in the last row is the sum of the entries for 40 and 7 above it. Students can check the entries in the last row by adding 47 successively on a calculator. This activity reinforces the connections between repeated addition of 47, skip-counting by 47, and skip-counting by both 40 and 7. Note that the table shows that 6 groups of 40 is 240, and 6 groups of 7 is 42, so 6 groups of (40 + 7) is 240 + 42.

Number of Iterations	1	2	3	4	5	6
Iteration Results for 40	40	80	120	160	200	240
Iteration Results for 7	7	14	21	28	35	42
Iteration Results for 47	47	94	141	188	235	282

One way you can relate skip-count tables to division is to ask, *What division problems can this table help you solve?* The above table can be used to solve two division problems: 282 ÷ 47 = 6 and 282 ÷ 6 = 47 [because the table shows that there are six 47s in 282].

Encouraging Place-Value Part Skip-Counting Using Problem Sequences

Another way to help students move to skip-counting multidigit numbers by place-value parts is to give sequences of problems that encourage place-value decomposition, as illustrated below. After students see how to use Problems A and B to figure out Problem C, try giving a problem similar to Problem C first and see if they can solve it by skip-counting place-value parts.

- **Problem A.** Suppose I have 4 containers with 3 candies in each container. How many candies do I have altogether? Skip-count by threes.
- **Problem B.** Suppose I have 4 containers with 20 candies in each container. How many candies do I have altogether? Skip-count by twenties.
- **Problem C.** Suppose I have 4 containers with 23 candies in each container. How many candies do I have altogether? How can your answers for Problems A and B help you with Problem C?

Similar problem sequences can be used for division.

- **Problem A.** Suppose I have 60 candies divided equally into 3 bags. How many candies are in each bag? Skip-count by twenties.
- **Problem B.** Suppose I have 9 candies divided equally into 3 bags. How many candies are in each bag? Skip-count by threes.
- **Problem C.** Suppose I have 69 candies divided equally into 3 bags. How many candies are in each bag? How can your answers for Problems A and B help you with Problem C?

Teaching Students at MD Level 2.4: Moving to Use of Properties

We now examine some activities for helping students extend their knowledge of number properties to multidigit numbers. Students must be proficient with their basic single-digit facts before they are encouraged to move to Level 3 for multidigit numbers.

Step 1. Mentally Multiplying and Dividing Multiples of Ten

MULTIPLYING To use the distributive property and place-value decomposition to multiply and divide multidigit numbers, students must first be fluent at mentally multiplying multiples of ten. To perform such multiplications, many students use the rule that says that to multiply multiples of ten, multiply the nonzero digits in the factors then append the number of zeros that occurred in the original factors. For example, to find 40×30, multiply 4×3 and append two 0s. As before, students start by discovering a pattern then move to understanding why the pattern occurs. Check students' knowledge of relevant basic facts before you begin.

Have students use a calculator to do the problems shown on **STUDENT SHEET 10** . Before they start, ask, *Can you predict the answer before entering the problem into the calculator? Can you find a pattern?* (Of course, to derive 30×5, a student must know the fact 3×5.) *What's the rule? How many zeros are in the original two numbers for a problem? How many zeros do you have to add to the answer after multiplying the nonzero parts of the numbers?*

$$10 \times 4 = \underline{\hspace{2cm}}$$
$$10 \times 6 = \underline{\hspace{2cm}}$$
$$30 \times 4 = \underline{\hspace{2cm}}$$
$$30 \times 6 = \underline{\hspace{2cm}}$$
$$30 \times 40 = \underline{\hspace{2cm}}$$
$$40 \times 80 = \underline{\hspace{2cm}}$$
$$50 \times 40 = \underline{\hspace{2cm}}$$

To help students see why this rule works, you can use the following explanation: *(5 × 30) = (5 groups of 3 tens) = 15 tens = 150.* (Students can use what they know about counting by tens to see that 15 tens = 150: 10, 20, 30, … 140, 150.)

The diagram below illustrates another way to help students understand the pattern.

10 × 5 = 10 rows of 5 = 5 columns of 10 = 5 tens = 50

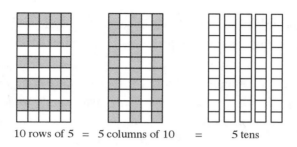

10 rows of 5   =   5 columns of 10   =   5 tens

10 × 15 = 10 rows of 15 = 15 columns of 10 = 15 tens = 150

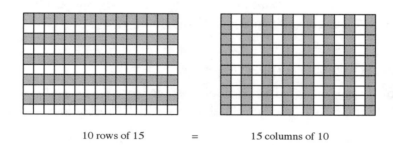

10 rows of 15   =   15 columns of 10

You can also give students sequences of problems like those below (see Part 2 on Student Sheet 10). The reasoning for Sequence A is: *5 times 3 tens = 15 tens = 150 ones, so 5 times 30 = 150.*

Sequence A

5 × (3 tens) = _____ tens = _____ ones

5 × 30 = _____

Sequence B

5 × (3 hundreds) = _____ hundreds = _____ ones

5 × 300 = _____

DIVIDING   Encourage students to extend the use of these mental strategies to division problems in which the dividend is a multiple of ten and the divisor is a single digit. For example, to find 240 ÷ 3, think 24 ÷ 3 equals 8 so 240 ÷ 3 equals 80. Use problem sequences similar to those for multiplication to help students understand this strategy. See **STUDENT SHEET 11** .

Sequence C

$$240 \div 3 = 24 \text{ tens} \div 3 = \underline{\hspace{1.5cm}} \text{ tens} = \underline{\hspace{1.5cm}} \text{ ones}$$

$$240 \div 3 = \underline{\hspace{1.5cm}}$$

Step 2. Intuitive Application of the Distributive Property in Physical Contexts

When students can think about a problem in terms of physical objects and actions, they usually can apply the distributive property informally without knowing its formal version. It just makes sense.

For example, in the problem, *There are 23 students. Each has 5 folders. How many folders are there altogether*, ask students: *How many folders do 20 students have? How much is 20 fives?* [100] *How many folders do 3 students have? How much is 3 fives?* [15] *So, how many folders do 23 students have? How much is 23 fives?* [100 +15 =115]

For division, consider the problem: *Suppose we want to give 20 pennies to each student. If we have 160 pennies, how many students can get 20 pennies?* Ask students, *How many 20s are in 100?* [5] *How many 20s are in 60?* [3] *So, how many 20s are in 160?* [5 + 3 = 8]. So, we can give 20 pennies to 8 students.

Applying Other Number Properties

After students have completed Steps 1 and 2, some work on the additional properties below will help them successfully transition to Level 3.1 reasoning.

THE COMMUTATIVE PROPERTY   Students can use a calculator to do the following pairs of problems. They should record all the problem statements and answers and look for and articulate any patterns they observe.

$$5 \times 3 = \underline{\hspace{2cm}} \qquad 3 \times 5 = \underline{\hspace{2cm}}$$
$$18 \times 6 = \underline{\hspace{2cm}} \qquad 6 \times 18 = \underline{\hspace{2cm}}$$
$$15 \times 23 = \underline{\hspace{2cm}} \qquad 23 \times 15 = \underline{\hspace{2cm}}$$
$$152 \times 238 = \underline{\hspace{2cm}} \qquad 238 \times 152 = \underline{\hspace{2cm}}$$

Note that division is *not* commutative. For example,

$$12 \div 6 = 2; 6 \div 12 = \frac{1}{2}$$

INVERSE RELATION BETWEEN MULTIPLICATION AND DIVISION   Students can use a calculator for the following two sets of four problems. After doing the first problem in each set, they should predict answers for the other three then check their predictions with the calculator. They should record the actual answers on the problem sheets then look for and explain patterns and relationships between problems.

$$18 \times 6 = \underline{\hspace{1cm}} \qquad 6 \times 18 = \underline{\hspace{1cm}} \qquad 108 \div 6 = \underline{\hspace{1cm}} \qquad 108 \div 18 = \underline{\hspace{1cm}}$$
$$23 \times 16 = \underline{\hspace{1cm}} \qquad 16 \times 23 = \underline{\hspace{1cm}} \qquad 368 \div 16 = \underline{\hspace{1cm}} \qquad 368 \div 23 = \underline{\hspace{1cm}}$$

Teaching Students at MD Level 3: From Place Value and the Distributive Property to Expanded Algorithms

First, students learn informal mental strategies for using the distributive property and place-value decomposition. Second, they formalize these informal mental strategies into expanded algorithms.

Teaching Students at MD Level 3.1: Moving to Place-Value Decomposition with Two Partial Products

Once students are fluent with multiplication facts involving multiples of ten, their next goal is to learn to use the distributive property and place value to decompose problems into two partial products [e.g., $5 \times 14 = (5 \times 10) + (5 \times 4)$]. One factor should have two digits; the other factor should have just one digit.

Start with problems in which students use place-value blocks or pictures of the blocks, as on **STUDENT SHEET 12** . The goal is for students to mentally compute each partial product then add the two partial products together. For instance, to find 4×23, students first mentally compute 4×20 to get 80, then mentally compute 4×3 to get 12, then add together 80 and 12 to get 92 as their answer. If a student cannot mentally compute one of the products, ask appropriate questions. For instance, if a student cannot mentally compute 4×20, ask *What is 4×2? How can you use that to find 4×20?* After students work on Student Sheet 12, be sure to give them opportunities to explain their answers to the whole class.

After students are comfortable with physical/visual problems, use **STUDENT SHEET 13** to encourage them to move to solving problems mentally, without being given pictures or blocks. As part of this mental reasoning, many students visualize what they would do with pictures or blocks. For students who have difficulty doing the problems mentally, encourage them to draw pictures that support those visualizations. If you are sure students understand tens and ones, you can show them how to represent tens and ones with abbreviated drawings. For instance, show students that they can draw the picture below to represent 4 groups of 13. But be vigilant—ask questions to determine if students really understand such drawings. For instance, circle the 4 tens-segments below and ask, *What do these mean? How many ones are in each ten?* Again, after students work on Student Sheet 13, be sure to give them opportunities to explain their answers to the whole class.

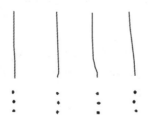

If drawing does not help students who are having difficulty, then return to problems using place-value blocks like those on Student Sheet 12. However, have students try to solve a problem mentally before giving them a picture or sets of place-value blocks. For instance, give the following problem.

Each bag contains 23 cubes. How many cubes are in 4 bags?

How many tens are in 23?

How many tens are in 4 bags of 2 ten-blocks?

How many cubes are in 4 bags of 20 cubes? $4 \times 20 =$ _____

How many cubes are in 4 bags of 3 cubes? $4 \times 3 =$ _____

How many cubes are in 4 bags of 23 cubes? $4 \times 23 =$ _____

If students have difficulty, show them the picture below and ask the same questions.

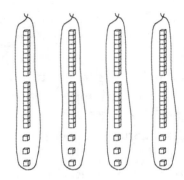

To see if students have made full sense of and can extend their work on Student Sheets 12 and 13, give them the candy bags problems on **STUDENT SHEET 14** ⬇ . Ask students to match the pictures with the statements and to write the letter of the picture that matches each statement. Be sure that students discuss as a class their answers on Student Sheet 14. The goal of the class discussions of Student Sheets 12–14 should be to make Level 3.2 reasoning explicit. We want students to see how to use, and be able to implement, the distributive property to decompose numbers by place value into two partial products.

Teaching Students at MD Level 3.2: Moving to Place-Value Decomposition with Four Partial Products

Using Arrays

Before students proceed to using the distributive property with four partial products, reassess their understanding of the array model for multiplication. You can use **STUDENT SHEET 15** ⬇ for this. If they have difficulty, revisit the instructional activities for students at Levels SD1.3 or 2.1 in Chapter 3.

Once students understand the use of arrays to represent single-digit multiplication problems, they can use graph paper divided into 10-by-10 sections to investigate the distributive property for multidigit multiplication. The problems on **STUDENT SHEET 16** 🔽 will help with this investigation. (Students should be able to do the partial-product calculations mentally.)

You can help students better understand the array representation shown in Problem 1 of Student Sheet 16 by showing them the even more expanded form below. This expanded form is derived from applying the distributive property to the expanded form of the product.

$$25 \times 34 = (10 + 10 + 5) \times (10 + 10 + 10 + 4)$$

	10	20	30	34
10	10 x 10	10 x 10	10 x 10	10 x 4
20	10 x 10	10 x 10	10 x 10	10 x 4
25	5 x 10	5 x 10	5 x 10	5x4

Once students fully understand the array representation shown in Problem 1, they can abbreviate the representation, without graph paper, as shown below. This representation leads nicely into the expanded form of the multiplication algorithm.

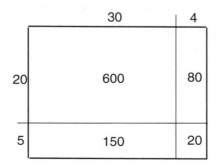

	30	4
20	600	80
5	150	20

Using Place-Value Blocks and Pictures

For students having difficulty understanding the array representations described above, you can use place-value blocks (or pictures of them) to provide another method for representing the distributive property using four partial products. Note that one number is represented along the left side and the other number along the top.

35
× 23

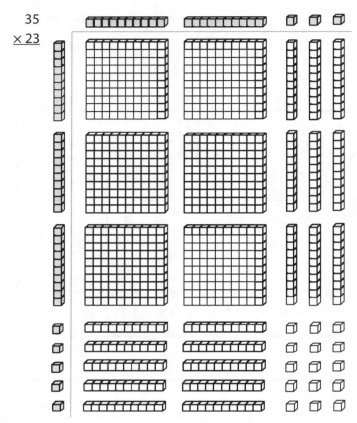

Ask students how this representation shows 35 × 23. Students should indicate which part of the representation corresponds to each partial product—(30 × 20), (30 × 3), (5 × 20), (5 × 3)—in the symbolic representation below.

$$35 \times 23 = (30 + 5) \times (20 + 3)$$
$$= (30 \times 20) + (30 \times 3) + (5 \times 20) + (5 \times 3)$$

Students using place-value blocks to represent this type of problem can draw a representation of their work as shown below.

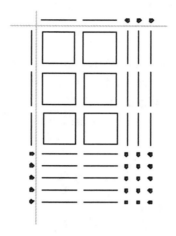

Teaching Students Who Are at MD Level 3.3: Moving from the Distributive Property to Expanded Algorithms

Once students understand and can implement MD Level 3.3 reasoning, we want them to learn expanded algorithms. These algorithms organize students' MD Level 3.3 reasoning to make computations more efficient and reliable. That is, it is common for students who have reached MD Level 3.3 reasoning to understand the process conceptually, but because this type of reasoning is complicated and places heavy demands on students' short-term memory, students sometimes lose track of what they are doing. Learning expanded algorithms that implement MD Level 3.3 reasoning organizes students' reasoning so that they are less likely to lose track of what they are doing and make mistakes.

Expanded Algorithm for Multiplication

The most common expanded multiplication algorithm is shown below. At first, it is useful for students to write the italicized partial products, but later, once you are sure they understand the procedure, they can omit these products.

$$
\begin{array}{r}
35 \\
\times\,23 \\
\hline
15 \quad \textit{(3} \times \textit{5)} \\
90 \quad \textit{(3} \times \textit{30)} \\
100 \quad \textit{(20} \times \textit{5)} \\
\underline{600} \quad \textit{(20} \times \textit{30)} \\
805
\end{array}
$$

When students have some proficiency with MD Level 3.3 reasoning (so they can correctly do problems like Problem 2 on Student Sheet 16), you can introduce the expanded algorithm shown above as an organized way of recording their Level 3.3 thinking, thus encouraging students to move to Level 4. In fact, for students who have achieved Level 3.3 reasoning, this expanded algorithm is just an organized way of using the distributive property with four partial products to perform the computation.

If students make place-value-related mistakes with the algorithm, don't just show them the correct way to do the algorithm. Ask questions that encourage them to see their place-value mistakes. For instance, consider a student who solved the problem 34 × 45 as shown below.

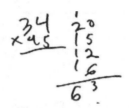

You might ask the student what the different digits represent. *What does the 3 in 34 mean: 3 or 30? What about the 4 in 45? Does that change your answer?* Students who have difficulty answering these questions may need more experience using MD Level 3.3 reasoning before moving to the algorithm. You can help them work through the reasoning with questions such as the following:

```
      34
    × 45
      20    (What is 5 × 4?)
     150    (What is 5 × 30?)
     160    (What is 40 × 4)
    1200    (What is 40 × 30)
    1530    (How much do we have altogether?)
```

For some students, it can be helpful to use a graphical representation like the one below.

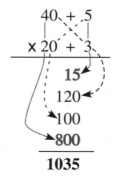

Expanded Algorithms for Division

One very useful expanded division algorithm builds on the idea of division as repeated subtraction. For instance, 928 ÷ 4 can be thought of as finding out how many times you can subtract 4 from 928. While repeatedly subtracting 4 may be a reasonable way to solve a problem like 28 ÷ 4, repeatedly subtracting 4 from 928 would be too tedious. In the expanded algorithm, students speed up the subtraction process by subtracting groups of 4s, especially groups based on multiples of ten.

For example, consider 128 ÷ 4. Instead of subtracting fours one at a time, we subtract 10 fours, which is 40. This leaves 128 – 40 = 88. Subtract 10 more fours, and we have 88 – 40 = 48 left. Subtract 10 more fours, and we have 8 left. Subtract 2 more fours, and we have a remainder of 0. How many fours did we subtract altogether? Writing out the process helps us keep track.

```
 128
– 40   (– 10 fours)
  88
– 40   (– 10 fours)
  48
– 40   (– 10 fours)
   8
–  8   (– 2 fours)
   0
```

We subtracted a total of 10 + 10 + 10 + 2 = 32 fours. So, 128 ÷ 4 = 32.

When we apply the same expanded algorithm to 928 ÷ 4, it might look like either solution below. The only difference between the two solutions is how efficient we are in subtracting groups of 4.

In Solution 1, we use familiar landmarks to determine how many fours to subtract at each stage. The total number of times 4 is subtracted from 928 is thus, 100 + 100 + 10 + 20 + 2.

In Solution 2, we subtract the maximum number of groups of 100 fours (200), then the maximum number groups of 10 fours (30), then the maximum number of fours left (2). The mental questioning that a student performs in implementing Solution 2 is as follows. 928 has a hundreds digit, so we start with hundreds. How many hundreds of times can we subtract 4 from 928? 100 times? Yes, that subtracts 400. 200 times? Yes, that subtracts 800. 300 times? No, because that subtracts 1200. So the maximum number of hundreds of times I can subtract 4 from 928 is 200. Now what is the maximum number of tens of times that I can subtract 4 from 128? Can I subtract ten 4s? Yes, that's 40. Twenty 4s? Yes, that's 80. Thirty 4s? Yes, that's 120. Forty 4s, no, because 160 is greater than 128. And so on.

This algorithm decomposes the dividend 928 into three parts, 800 + 120 + 8, corresponding to a place-value decomposition of the quotient into the sum of three partial quotients, 200 + 30 + 2: (800 ÷ 4, 120 ÷ 4, 8 ÷ 4).

Solution 1 is not maximally efficient because it has two partial quotients each for hundreds and tens, but this lack of efficiency makes this form of the algorithm easier for students to use because their estimates do not have to be perfect. For each step, they can remove the number of fours from 928 that makes sense to them rather than having to estimate the maximum number they can remove at once.

Solution 1	Solution 2
$$\begin{array}{r} 928 \\ -400 \quad (100 \times 4) \\ \hline 528 \\ -400 \quad (100 \times 4) \\ \hline 128 \\ -40 \quad (10 \times 4) \\ \hline 88 \\ -80 \quad (20 \times 4) \\ \hline 8 \\ -8 \quad (2 \times 4) \\ \hline 0 \end{array}$$ $100 + 100 + 10 + 20 + 2 = 232$	$$\begin{array}{r} 928 \\ -800 \quad (200 \times 4) \\ \hline 128 \\ -120 \quad (30 \times 4) \\ \hline 8 \\ -8 \quad (2 \times 4) \\ \hline 0 \end{array}$$ $200 + 30 + 2 = 232$

You can help students understand the reasoning behind Solution 2 by modeling conceptually meaningful language, such as the following:

How many times can 4 be subtracted from 928?

Step 1. Subtract four 100 times, that's 400; subtract four 200 times, that's 800; if we try to subtract four 300 times, that would be too much (1200 is greater than 928). So, it's 200. Subtracting four 200 times means subtracting 800, so there's 128 left.

Step 2. Now we subtract fours from 128. Subtract four 10 times, that's 40; subtract four 20 times, that's 80; subtract four 30 times, that's 120; subtracting four 40 times would be too much (160 is greater than 128). So, it's 30. Subtracting four 30 times means subtracting 120, so there's 8 left.

Step 3. Now we subtract fours from 8. Subtracting four 2 times means subtracting 8, so there's 0 left, or no remainder.

The total number of times 4 is subtracted from 928 is 200 + 30 + 2, or 232. So, 928 divided by 4 is 232.

Teaching Students at MD Level 4: Moving from Expanded to Traditional Algorithms

The traditional algorithm for multiplying two numbers is shown below.

$$
\begin{array}{r}
\overset{\scriptstyle 1}{4}5 \\
\times\ 23 \\
\hline
135 \\
90 \\
\hline
1035
\end{array}
$$

Most adults and students, when describing this algorithm, don't mention the place value of the digits:

"*3 times 5 is 15, write the 5 under the 3, carry the 1* [writes 1 above 4]. *3 times 4 is 12 plus 1 is 13* [writes 13 starting under 2]. *2 times 5 is 10, write the 0* [under the 3], *carry the 1* [writing another 1 above 4]. *2 times 4 is 8 plus 1 is 9* [writing the 9 under the 1]."

In this description, the phrase "3 times 4 is 12" really means 3 times 40 is 120; the place values of the 4 and the 12 are not explicitly mentioned in the words used to describe the manipulations. The traditional algorithm reduces multiplying multidigit numbers to single-digit multiplication and appropriate spatial positioning. Although this spatial positioning is determined by place value, the place values are not explicitly named while performing the algorithm, so students often learn this algorithm by rote.

To help students make sense of the traditional algorithm, it must be explicitly related, piece by piece, to the expanded algorithm (which students should learn first), as illustrated by the questioning sequence below.

I've written two ways to find 45 times 23 on the chalkboard. How can you use the one on the left to explain where the numbers come from in the one on the right?

$$
\begin{array}{r}
45 \\
\times\ 23 \\
\hline
15 \\
120 \\
100 \\
800 \\
\hline
1035
\end{array}
\qquad\qquad
\begin{array}{r}
45 \\
\times\ 23 \\
\hline
135 \\
90 \\
\hline
1035
\end{array}
$$

Students: *The 135* [pointing to 135 in the traditional algorithm] *comes from the 120 + 15* [pointing to the 15 and 120 in the expanded algorithm].

Teacher: *And where do the 120 and 15 come from?*

Students: *From multiplying 45 times 3. 45 is 40 + 5.*

Teacher: *How about the 90 in the one on the right? Is it really a 90?*

Students: *It's 90 tens, so 900. It's the same as the 100 + 800 in the other one.*

Teacher: *Where do the 100 and 800 come from?*

Students: *From multiplying 45 times 20 because 45 equals 40 + 5.*

During the class discussion, use arrows to show the connections between the corresponding parts of the two algorithms.

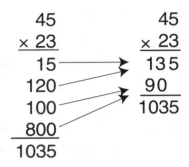

The same kind of connection can be made between the expanded and traditional division algorithms. Consider the two solutions to the same division problem shown below. Solution 1 is an implementation of the expanded algorithm introduced in MD Level 4. Solution 2 is an implementation of the traditional algorithm.

Solution 1: Expanded Algorithm	Solution 2: Traditional Algorithm
4)928 − 800 (200 × 4) 128 − 120 (30 × 4) 8 − 8 (2 × 4) 0 200 + 30 + 2 = 232	232 4)928 −8 12 −12 08 −8 0

Both the expanded and traditional algorithms can be interpreted as determining how many times four can be subtracted from 928 or how many fours are in 928. You can help students make sense of the traditional algorithm by carefully connecting it to the expanded algorithm. Ask students to use Solution 1 to explain the numbers in Solution 2. A student who understands the relationship might answer:

Student: *The numbers match up. The first 2 in Solution 2 is the 200 in Solution 1. The 3 in Solution 2 is the 30 in Solution 1, and the last 2 is just the 2. And the minus 8 [in Solution 2] is the minus 800 over here [Solution 1]; the minus 12 is the minus 120 over here, and the minus 8 is the minus 8.*

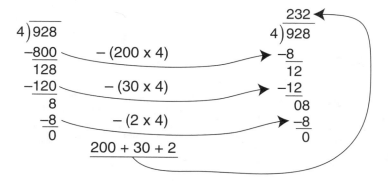

Teacher: *Why is the first 2 in Solution 2 the same as the 200 in Solution 1?*

Student: *Solution 1 says that 4 can be subtracted from 928 two hundred times. In Solution 2, when you say that there are 2 fours in 9, you really mean that there are 200 fours in 900 because the first 2 and the 9 are in the hundreds place. And you put the 8 in the hundreds place because 200 fours equals 800.*

Though there are other ways to make the traditional division algorithm meaningful for students, CBA uses the expanded subtraction algorithm shown above because it supports the powerful learning progression from MD Level 3.3 through Level 4 to Level 5.

Glossary of Key Terms

Algorithm—a precisely specified sequence of steps for finding solutions to a specific type of problem.

Arithmetic Operation—a well-defined rule for associating two numbers with a third number; for instance, the addition operation associates the pair of numbers 3 and 5 with the number 8.

Composite Unit—a collection of things that has been mentally combined and treated as a unit; for example, when skip-counting by three—3, 6, 9, 12—three is the composite unit.

Iterate—to repeat and accumulate an object or set of objects, quantity, or action in an organized manner; for instance, to find 5×4, you can iterate the number 4 five times by skip-counting: 4, 8, 12, 16, 20; or you can iterate a set of 4 objects 5 times to see that 5×4 equals 20.

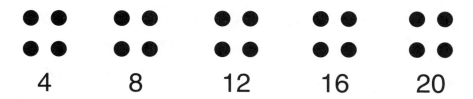

Place-Value Decomposition of a Number—to express a number as a sum of tens and ones; hundreds, tens, and ones; and so on; for example, we can decompose 458 into $400 + 50 + 8$.

Appendix

CBA Assessment Tasks for Multiplication and Division

$\times \div$

These problems can be used in individual interviews with children or in class as instructional activities. However, no matter which use you choose, it is critical to get the students to write and describe or discuss their strategies. Only then can you use the CBA levels to interpret students' responses and decide on needed instruction.

Guide for Interviewing Students with CBA Tasks

The purpose of interviewing students with CBA tasks is to determine how they are reasoning and, more specifically, to determine what CBA levels of reasoning they are using for the tasks.

What CBA staff said to students before interviews is shown below.

> "I am going to give you some problems. I would like to know what you think while you solve these problems. So, tell me everything you think as you do the problems. Try to think out loud. Tell me what you are doing and why you are doing it. I will also ask you questions to help me understand what you are thinking. For instance, if you say something that I don't understand, I will ask you questions about it."

If you don't understand what a student is saying, you could ask, "I don't understand. Could you explain that again?" Or "What do you mean by such-and-such?" Try to get students to explain in their own words rather than paraphrasing what you think they mean and asking if they agree. If, during an interview, a student asked whether his or her answers are correct, we told him or her that, for this interview, it does not really matter. We are interested in what he or she thinks.

Students responded to our request to "think out loud" in two ways. Many students were quite capable of thinking out loud as they solved problems. They told us what they were thinking and doing as they thought about it and did it. Other students, however, seemed unable to think aloud as they completed problems. They worked in silence but then gave us detailed accounts of what they did *after* they finished doing it.

The following tasks cover a large range of reasoning about multiplying and dividing whole numbers. You probably will not want to give all the problems to your students, at least at one time. For students in Grades 2 and 3, you should select from Problems 1–6 depending on your curriculum. For students in Grades 4 and 5, you should select from Problems 3–14. Of course, you can alter these suggestions based on your curriculum.

Many of the problems have notes that indicate particular aspects of students' reasoning emphasized by the problems.

Additional assessment tasks may be downloaded from this book's website, www .heinemann.com/products/E04344.aspx. (Click on the "Companion Resources" tab.)

Teacher Notes for Individual Tasks

Problem 1: Show students a container as you read the problem aloud. If students cannot do the problem, give them 4 containers and 20 cubes to see if they can act out the problem.

Problem 2: Show students a container as you read the problem aloud. If students cannot do the problem, give them 6 containers and 20 cubes to see if they can act out the problem.

1. I have 4 containers. There are 3 cubes in each container.
   How many cubes are there altogether?

2. I have 20 cubes. I want to put them into containers so there are 5 cubes in each container.
   How many containers do I need?

Name _____   Date _____

3. $6 \times 8 =$ _____

4. A carton contains 12 eggs. Emily has 5 cartons.
How many eggs does Emily have altogether?

5. Mary has 84 cookies. She wants to divide them equally among 4 people. How many cookies does each person get?

6. $10 \times 6 =$ _____

7. $20 \times 8 =$ _____

8. $10 \times 37 =$ _____

9. $40 \times 60 =$ _____

10. Jon was solving the problem
   $5 \times 23 =$ _____
He wrote
   $5 \times 20 = 100$
   $5 \times 3 = 15$
How could he use the information he wrote to find 5 times 23?

Use Jon's method to solve $8 \times 32 =$ _____

Name _____   Date _____

11. $128 \div 8 =$ _____

12. $45 \times 23 =$ _____

13. The answers to some or all of the problems below can be added to find the answer to 16×57.

$6 \times 7 =$

$6 \times 50 =$

$10 \times 7 =$

$10 \times 50 =$

Circle the problems whose answers should be added to find the answer to 16×57. Try to figure this out without calculating any multiplications.

Name _____   Date _____

14. Part of what Mary wrote to solve the problem 161 ÷ 7 = _____ is shown below.

```
  7 )161
   − 70    7 × 10
     91
   − 70    7 × 10
     21
   − 21    7 × 3
      0
```

What should Mary do next to find her answer? Why?

Why did Mary subtract 70?

What does the 91 mean?

CBA Levels for Each Task

The descriptions below show sample student responses at various levels of sophistication.

Single-Digit Multiplication and Division

The first set of problems are designed to determine how students reason about single-digit multiplication and division.

PROBLEM 1

I have 4 containers. There are 3 cubes in each container. How many cubes are there altogether?

SD Level 0: Student says, "I don't know."

Or student says, "There's 7."

SD Level 1.1: Student makes 4 sets of 3 cubes then counts cubes by ones.

Or student draws 4 sets of 3 squares then counts squares by ones.

Without visual material, student miscounts.

SD Level 1.2: Student says, "*[Raises one finger]* 1, 2, 3; *[raises second finger]* 4, 5, 6; *[raises third finger]* 7, 8, 9; *[raises fourth finger]* 10, 11, 12."

SD Level 1.3: Student says, "1 group is 3 *[puts up one finger]*, 2 groups is 6 *[puts up a second finger]*; 7 *[puts up a third finger]*, 8 *[puts up a fourth finger]*."

SD Level 2.1: Student says "I know that 3 + 3 is 6, then 3 + 3 is 6 again, so then I added the 6s together and got 12."

Or student says, "*[extends one finger]* 3, *[extends another finger]* 6, *[extends another finger]* 9, *[extends another finger]* 10, 11, 12. 12 cubes."

SD Level 2.2: Student skip-counts 2, 4, 6, 8 plus 4 more equals 12.

SD Level 2.3: Student skip-counts 3, 6, 9, 12. There are 12 cubes.

SD Level 2.4: Student says, "Two groups is 6, so 4 groups is 12."

SD Level 3.1: Student says, "12; you times 4 by 3. *[Teacher: How did you figure that out?]* I just knew it."

SD Level 3.2: Student says, "3 times 3 is 9, plus 3 more is 12."

PROBLEM 2

I have 20 cubes. I want to put them into containers so there are 5 cubes in each container. How many containers do I need?

SD Level 0: Student says, "I don't know."

Or student says, "There's 15."

SD Level 1.1: Student gets 20 cubes and puts them into 4 sets of 5 then counts the 4 sets by ones.

Or student draws 20 squares and circles 4 sets of 5 then counts circled groups.

Without visual material, student miscounts.

SD Level 1.2: Student says, "*[Raises one finger]* 1, 2, 3, 4, 5; *[raises second finger]* 6, 7, 8, 9, 10; *[raises third finger]* 11, 12, 13, 14 15; *[raises fourth finger]* 16, 17, 18, 19, 20."

SD Level 1.3: Student says, "*[puts out finger pattern of 5]* 5; *[puts another pattern of 5]* 6; *[puts another pattern of 5]* 7; *[puts another pattern of 5]* 8."

SD Level 2.1: Student says, "5 + 5 is 10; + 5 equals 15, + 5 equals 20. That's four 5s."

Or student counts 5, 10, 15; 16, 17, 18, 19, 20; I did four 5s.

SD Level 2.2: Not applicable. (There is only one place value part in 20, and that is 20.)

SD Level 2.3: Student says, "If I count by fives—5, 10, 15, 20—four times, I get 20. So, I need 4 containers."

SD Level 2.4: Student says, "Two groups is 10, so 4 groups is 20."

SD Level 3.1: Student says, "I know that 20 divided by 5 is 4."

SD Level 3.2: Student says, "I know that 5 times 4 is 20; so, 20 divided by 5 is 4."

PROBLEM 3

$$6 \times 8 = \underline{\hspace{2cm}}$$

SD Level 0: Student says, "I don't know."

Or student says, "There's 14."

SD Level 1.1: Student makes 6 sets of 8 cubes then counts cubes by ones.

Or student draws 6 sets of 8 dots then counts dots by ones.

Without visual material, student miscounts.

SD Level 1.2: Student says, "*[Raises one finger]* 1, 2, 3, 4, 5, 6, 7, 8; *[raises second finger]* 9, 10, 11, 12, 13, 14 15, 16; and so on." *[There is a high probability of error in using this procedure with these numbers.]*

SD Level 1.3: Student skip-counts incorrectly 8, 16, 22, 30, 36, 42.

SD Level 2.1: Student writes out 8 + 8 = 16; 16 + 8 = 24; 24 + 8 = 32; 32 + 8 = 40; 40 + 8 = 48.

Or student counts 8, 16, 24; 25, 26, 27, 28, 29, 30, 31, 32; 40; 48.

SD Level 2.2: Student says, "Eight fives is 5, 10, 15, 20, 25, 30, 35, 40. Plus 8 equals 48."

SD Level 2.3: Student skip-counts 8, 16, 24, 32, 40, 48.

Or student skip-counts 6, 12, 18, 24, 30, 36, 42, 48.

SD Level 2.4: Student says, "2 sixes is 12. So, 6 sixes is 12, 24, 36."

SD Level 3.1: Student says, "6 times 8 equals 48. I just remember it."

SD Level 3.2: Student says, "8 times 5 is 40, plus one more 8 is 48."

Multidigit Multiplication and Division

The next set of problems are designed to determine how students reason about two-digit multiplication and division. If students use the traditional algorithm on these problems, you must ask additional questions to determine their CBA level of reasoning. See Chapter 2, page 62, for more on this kind of questioning.

PROBLEM 4

A carton contains 12 eggs. Emily has 5 cartons. How many eggs does Emily have altogether?

MD Level 1.1: Student makes 12 sets of 5 cubes then counts cubes by ones.

Or student draws 12 sets of 5 squares then counts squares by ones.

Without visual material, student miscounts.

MD Level 1.2: Student says, "1, 2, 3, 4, 5 *[puts up one finger]*; 6, 7, 8, 9, 10 *[puts up another finger]*; ... 56, 57, 58, 59, 60 *[puts up a twelfth finger]*. 60 eggs."

MD Level 1.3: Student skip-counts incorrectly 12, 24, 29, 34, 39.

MD Level 1.4: *[Student counts the number of cubes on 1 ten-block then puts 1 ten-block together with 2 unit cubes]* 12. *[She then makes 4 more sets of 1 ten-block and 2 ones then counts all the cubes by ones]* 1, 2 ... 60.

MD Level 2.1: Student says, "12 + 12 = 24. 24 + 12 = 36. 36 + 12 = 48."

Or student counts 12, 24, 36, 48, 49, 50, ... 59, 60.

MD Level 2.2: Student skip-counts 24, 48, 60.

MD Level 2.3: Student skip-counts 12, 24, 36, 48, 60.

MD Level 2.4: Student skip-counts 10, 20, 30, 40, 50. 2, 4, 6, 8, 10. 50 and 10 is 60.

MD Level 3.1: Student says, "5 times 5 is 25; 5 times 5 again is 25; and 5 times 2 is 10. Add those together, it is 60."

MD Level 3.2: Student says, "Five tens is 50. Five 2s equals 10. 50 plus 10 equals 60."

MD Level 3.3: Not applicable. (Level 3.3 only applies to problems having two 2-digit numbers.)

MD Level 4: *[Student uses a written expanded algorithm.]*

$$
\begin{array}{r}
12 \\
\times\,5 \\
\hline
10 \\
\underline{50} \\
60
\end{array}
$$

MD Level 5: Student uses traditional multiplication algorithm and, when questioned, explains it using the expanded algorithm.

PROBLEM 5

Mary has 84 cookies. She wants to divide them equally among 4 people. How many cookies does each person get?

MD Level 1.1: Student counts out 84 cubes then puts them one by one into 4 sets. She then counts the 21 cubes in one set by ones and gives an answer of 21.

Or student draws 4 circles and puts dots in the circles one by one as she counts to 84. She then counts 21 dots in one circle.

MD Level 1.2: Student says, "1, 2, 3, 4 *[raises one finger]*; 5, 6, 7, 8 *[raises a second finger]*; 9, 10, 11, 12 *[raises a third finger]* … 77, 78, 79, 80 *[raises a twentieth finger]*; 81, 82, 83, 84 *[raises a twenty-first finger]*. I did 21 fingers; so it's 21 cookies for each person."

MD Level 1.3: Student says, "*[Puts up ten fingers, one at a time]* 4, 8, 12 … 36, 40. That's 10. *[Puts up ten fingers, one at a time]* 10, 14, 18, 22 … 46, 50. That's 20. I'm confused."

MD Level 1.4: Student makes 84 from 8 ten-blocks and 4 ones. Give one of these to each person *[deals out 4 ten-blocks]*. Give one more of these to each person *[deals out 4 ten-blocks]*. Now each person gets one of these *[ones]*. So, each person gets 21.

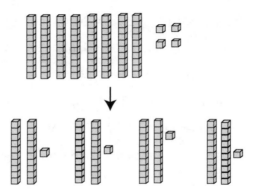

MD Level 2.1: Student says, "84 – 4 = 80; 80 – 4 = 76; 76 – 4 = 72 … 4 – 4 = 0." *[Student counts 21 subtractions and says the answer is 21.]*

MD Level 2.2: Student says, "4 plus 4 equals 8, 8 plus 8 equals 16. So that's 4 fours. 16 and 16 is 32, that's 8 fours. 64 makes 18 fours, plus 16 equals 80 makes 20 fours, plus one more four makes 21."

MD Level 2.3: Student says, "4, 8, 12, 16 … 80, 84 *[using fingers to keep track of the number of fours].*"

MD Level 2.4: Student says, "*[After drawing the following picture]* I put 10 in each group, then 10 more, then 1. So, each person gets 21 cookies."

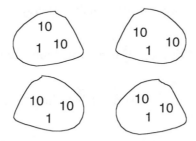

MD Level 3.1: Student says, "20 divided by 4 is 5. 20 divided by 4 is 5. 20 divided by 4 is 5. 24 divided by 4 is 6. So add them up: 5 + 5 + 5 + 6 = 21."

MD Level 3.2: Student says, "80 divided by 4 equals 20. 4 divided by 4 equals 1. 20 plus 1 equals 21."

MD Level 3.3: Not applicable. (Level 3.3 only applies to problems having two 2-digit numbers.)

MD Level 4: *[Student uses a written expanded algorithm.]*

```
  4)84
  – 80    –(20 × 4)
    4
  – 4     –(1 × 4)
    0     21
```

MD Level 5: Student uses traditional division algorithm and, when questioned, explains it using the expanded algorithm or base-ten blocks.

Be sure to determine if students can do problems such as Problems 6 to 10 mentally. (If they cannot do the problems mentally, let them use whatever method they choose.)

PROBLEM 6

$10 \times 6 =$ _____

MD Level 1.1: Student counts or draws 10 groups of 6 objects. She then counts from 1 to 60 by ones.

MD Level 1.2: Student shows ten fingers and counts 1–10, shows ten more fingers and counts 11–20 … shows ten more fingers and counts 51–60.

MD Level 1.3: Student skip-counts incorrectly 6, 12, 18, 28, 38, 48, 58.

MD Level 1.4: Student grabs 6 ten-blocks and says 60.

MD Level 2.1: Student repeatedly adds 10 or 6 to make 60, or does partial skip-count, supplemented by counting by ones: 6, 12, 18, 24, 30, 36; 37, 38 … 60 *[often with errors]*.

MD Level 2.2: Student says, "10, 20 that's 2 tens. So, 40 is 4 tens, and 60 is 6 tens."

MD Level 2.3: Student skip-counts 10, 20, 30, 40, 50, 60. Or student skip-counts by 6 to 60.

MD Level 2.4: Not applicable. (For this problem, Level 2.4 is the same as Level 2.3.)

MD Level 3.1: Student says, "6 times 1 is 6 then "add" a zero *[This is the zero rule of multiplication]*."

MD Level 3.2, 3.3: Not applicable.

MD Level 4: Student says, "6 times 10 is 60." *[Student uses an expanded algorithm.]*

$$\begin{array}{r} 10 \\ \times\,6 \\ \hline 60 \end{array}$$

MD Level 5: Student says, "*[using traditional algorithm]* 6 times 0 is 0; 6 times 1 is 6; so, 60 is the answer." *[But student can explain why he used these steps using place-value concepts.]*

$$\begin{array}{r} 10 \\ \times\,6 \\ \hline 60 \end{array}$$

PROBLEM 7

$$20 \times 8 = \underline{\hspace{2cm}}$$

MD Level 1.1: Student counts or draws 8 groups of 20 objects. She then counts from 1 to 160 by ones.

MD Level 1.2: Student shows ten fingers 16 times, counting by ones to 160.

MD Level 1.3: Student skip-counts incorrectly 20, 40, 60, 80, 100, 110, 120, 130.

MD Level 1.4: Student grabs 16 ten-blocks, two at a time. She puts 9 ten-blocks together and says 90 but then stops because she does not understand the tens-to-ones correspondence for numbers in the hundreds.

MD Level 2.1: Student repeatedly adds 20 or 8 to make 160 but may make a mistake in some of the additions.

Or student does partial skip-count, supplemented by counting by ones: 8, 16, 24, 32, 40, 48, 56, 64; 65, 66, … *[often with errors].*

MD Level 2.2: Student skip-counts by ten 16 times.

MD Level 2.3: Student skip-counts 20, 40, 60, 80, 100 120, 140, 160.

MD Level 2.4: Not applicable.

MD Level 3.1: Student says, "8 times 2 is 16; then "add" a zero." *[This is the zero property of multiplication.]*

Or student says, "8 times 10 is 80, plus another 8 times 10 is 160." *[Student uses an expanded algorithm.]*

MD Level 3.2, 3.3: Not applicable.

MD Level 4: Student says, "8 times 20 is 160."

```
  20
× 8
 160
```

MD Level 5: Student says, "*[using traditional algorithm]* 8 times 0 is 0; 8 times 2 is 16; so, 160 is the answer." *[But student can explain why he used these steps using place-value concepts.]*

```
  20
× 8
 160
```

PROBLEM 8

$$10 \times 37 = \text{_____}$$

MD Level 1.1–1.4: Not applicable. (Do not give problems with such large factors to students who are counting by ones.)

MD Level 2.1: Student adds 37 ten times.

MD Level 2.2: Not applicable.

MD Level 2.3: Student skip-counts by tens 37 times.

MD Level 2.4: Student skip-counts by 30 ten times getting 300, skip-counts by 7 ten times getting 70, and adds 300 and 70.

MD Level 3.1: Student says, "37 times 1 is 37 then "add" a zero." *[This is the zero property of multiplication.]*

Or 10 times 20 is 200; 10 times 17 is 170; 200 plus 170 is 370.

MD Level 3.2: Student says, "10 times 30 equals 300; 10 times 7 equals 70; 300 plus 70 equals 370."

MD Level 3.3: Not applicable.

MD Level 4: Student says, "10 times 30 equals 300; 10 times 7 equals 70; 300 plus 70 equals 370." *[Student uses a written expanded algorithm.]*

```
    37
  × 10
   300
    70
   370
```

MD Level 5: Student says, "*[using traditional algorithm]* 0 times 37 is 0; put a 0. 1 times 7 is 7; 1 times 3 is 3" *[But student can explain why he used these steps using place-value concepts.]*

```
    37
  × 10
   370
```

PROBLEM 9

$$40 \times 60 = \underline{\hspace{2cm}}$$

Problems with such large factors are too tedious to solve at MD Levels 1 and 2. So, if a student starts adding or skip-counting by 60, ask the student what she intends to do, then explain that all you need to know is how she would do the problem. She does not need to finish. Then ask her if there is another way she can do the problem.

MD Level 1.1–2.4: Not applicable.

MD Level 3.1: Student says, "6 times 4 is 24; then "add" two zeros." *[This is the zero property of multiplication.]*

MD Level 3.2: Not applicable.

MD Level 3.3: Not applicable.

MD Level 4: Student says, "40 times 60 equals 2400." *[Student uses a written expanded algorithm.]*

```
    40
  × 60
  2400
```

MD Level 5: Student says, "*[using traditional algorithm]* 0 times 0 is 0; put a 0. 0 times 4 is 0; put a 0. 6 times 0 is 0; put a 0. 6 times 4 equals 24; put 24. *[But student can explain why he used these steps using place-value concepts.]*"

```
    40
  × 60
    00
   240
  2400
```

The following problem helps you determine if students possess an initial understanding of how to use the distributive property and place-value decomposition for multiplying multidigit numbers.

PROBLEM 10

Jon was solving the problem

$$5 \times 23 = \underline{\hspace{1.5cm}}$$

He wrote

$$5 \times 20 = 100$$
$$5 \times 3 = 15$$

How could he use the information he wrote to find 5 times 23?

Use Jon's method to solve $8 \times 32 = \underline{\hspace{1.5cm}}$

This problem is used to explicitly assess whether students are capable of MD Level 3.2 reasoning, so it is not applicable to MD Levels 1.1 to 3.1.

MD Level 1.1–3.1: Not applicable.

MD Level 3.2: Students who are capable of Level 3.2 reasoning will say that Jon should add 100 and 15 "because you are multiplying 5 times 23 and 23 is 20 plus 3."

Students who understand Level 3.2 reasoning will say that to solve the problem 8 times 32 using Jon's method, you should do the following:

$$8 \times 30 = 240$$
$$8 \times 2 = 16$$
$$240 + 16 = 256$$

MD Level 3.3: Not applicable.

MD Level 4: Students who are reasoning at Level 4 might say that Jon is or should be using their [expanded] algorithm, but he is not writing it the way they do. Such students might find the product of 8 times 32 using the expanded multiplication algorithm.

$$
\begin{array}{r}
32 \\
\times 8 \\
\hline
16 \\
240 \\
\hline
256 \\
\end{array}
$$

MD Level 5: Students who are reasoning at Level 5 might do the problems using a traditional algorithm. But they will explain that Jon is doing the exact same thing, but he is writing all the steps out.

PROBLEM 11

$$128 \div 8 = \underline{\hspace{1cm}}$$

MD Level 1.1: Student counts or draws 128 objects, puts them into groups of 8, then counts the number of groups by ones.

MD Level 1.2: This problem is impractical at this level.

MD Level 1.3: Student skip-counts incorrectly 8, 16, 24, 32, 40, 48, 56, 64, 72, 80, 90, 101, 112.

MD Level 1.4: Not applicable.

MD Level 2.1: Student either repeatedly subtracts 8, starting at 128, or repeatedly adds 8 until getting 128. The answer is the number of times 8 is added or subtracted.

MD Level 2.2: This problem is impractical at this level.

MD Level 2.3: Student skip-counts by 8s until reaching 128, keeping track of counts perhaps by raising fingers.

MD Level 2.4: Not applicable. (There's just one place-value part.)

MD Level 3.1: Student says, "$80 \div 8 = 10$. $48 \div 8 = 6$. $10 + 6 = 16$."

MD Level 3.2: Student says, "10 times 8 equals 80. 6 times 8 equals 48. $10 + 6$ equals 16."

MD Level 3.3: Technically, Level 3.3 is not applicable. The closest kind of reasoning, which is very difficult, is the following: $100 \div 8 = 12r4$. $20 \div 8 = 2r4$. Add the remainders: $(4 + 4) \div 8 = 1$. $8 \div 8 = 1$. Add $12 + 2 + 1 + 1 = 16$.

MD Level 4: *[Student uses a written expanded algorithm.]*

```
8 )128
  - 80    -(10 × 8)
    48
  - 48    -(6 × 8)
     0     16
```

MD Level 5: Student uses traditional division algorithm and, when questioned, explains it using the expanded algorithm or base-ten blocks.

```
     16
8 )128
   -8
   48
  -48
    0
```

PROBLEM 12

$$45 \times 23 = \underline{\qquad}$$

This problem is impractical to solve with MD Level 1 reasoning.

Also, problems with such large factors are very tedious to solve at MD Level 2. So, if a student starts adding or skip-counting by 45 or 23, ask the student what she intends to do, then explain that all you need to know is how she would do the problem. She does not need to finish. Then ask her if there is another way she can do the problem.

MD Level 1.1–2.4: Not applicable.

MD Level 3.1: Student says, "45 times 10 is 450. 45 times another 10 is 450; that's 900. 45 times 3 is 120 plus 15. So, it's 1035."

MD Level 3.2: Student says, "45 times 20 is 900. 45 times 3 is 135. So, it's 1035."

MD Level 3.3: Student writes 40 times 20 equals 800. 40 times 3 equals 120. 5 times 20 equals 100. 5 times 3 equals 15. 800 + 120 + 100 + 15 equals 800, 900, 1000, 1020, 1035.

MD Level 4: *[Student uses a written expanded algorithm.]*

```
   45
 × 23
   15
  120
  100
  800
 1035
```

MD Level 5: Student uses traditional algorithm but can explain why he used these steps using place-value concepts.

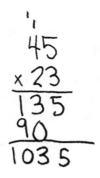

Problem 13 assesses whether students understand how to multiply multidigit numbers by decomposing them by place value into 4 partial products. So, this task assesses directly if students are capable of MD Level 3.3 reasoning. Keep in mind that Level 3.3 reasoning is a prerequisite for Level 4 and Level 5 reasoning.

PROBLEM 13

The answers to some or all of the problems below can be added to find the answer to 16×57.

$$6 \times 7 =$$
$$6 \times 50 =$$
$$10 \times 7 =$$
$$10 \times 50 =$$

Circle the problems whose answers should be added to find the answer to 16×57. Try to figure this out without calculating any multiplications.

MD Level 1.1–3.2: Not applicable.

MD Level 3.3: Student circles all four answers. If asked why, student can explain the process using an array model.

MD Level 4: Student circles all four answers saying that these are the four multiplications you do when you use the expanded algorithm.

$$
\begin{array}{r}
16 \\
\times\, 57 \\
\hline
42 \\
70 \\
300 \\
\underline{500} \\
\end{array}
$$

MD Level 5: Students who are reasoning at Level 5 will explain that doing the problem with the algorithm is the exact same thing as above but the above shows all the steps. They would be able to explain how the four multiplications above appear in the traditional algorithm.

Problem 14 assesses whether students understand an expanded division algorithm. Understanding this algorithm implementation requires MD Level 3 reasoning applied to division. That is, students must understand that:

$$161 \div 7 = (70 + 70 + 21) \div 7 = (70 \div 7) + (70 \div 7) + (21 \div 7)$$

or that:

$$(7 \times 10) + (7 \times 10) + (7 \times 3) = 7 \times 23 = 161$$

PROBLEM 14

Part of what Mary wrote to solve the problem $161 \div 7 =$ is shown below.

```
7 )161
  -70    7 × 10
   91
  -70    7 × 10
   21
  -21    7 × 3
    0
```

What should Mary do next to find her answer? Why?

Why did Mary subtract 70?

What does the 91 mean?

MD Level 1.1–2.4: Not applicable.

MD Level 3: Student says to add 10, 10, and 3 because you subtracted 10 sevens, 10 sevens, and 3 sevens, which total 23 sevens. Student can give reasonable answers to the other two questions.

MD Levels 4–5: Student says to add 10, 10, and 3 and can give reasonable answers to the other two questions. Student uses the following ideas as justifications.

$$161 \div 7 = (70 + 70 + 21) \div 7 = (70 \div 7) + (70 \div 7) + (21 \div 7)$$

or

$$(7 \times 10) + (7 \times 10) + (7 \times 3) = 7 \times 23 = 161$$

References

×÷

Baroody, A. J., and Ginsburg, H. P. (1990). Children's Learning: A Cognitive View. In R. B. Davis, C. A. Maher, and N. Noddings (Eds.), Constructivist Views on the Teaching and Learning of Mathematics. *Journal for Research in Mathematics Education Monograph Number 4* (pp. 51–64). Reston, VA: National Council of Teachers of Mathematics.

Battista, M. T. (February 1999). The Mathematical Miseducation of America's Youth: Ignoring Research and Scientific Study in Education. *Phi Delta Kappan*, *80*(6): 424–433.

Battista, M. T. (2001). How Do Children Learn Mathematics? Research and Reform in Mathematics Education. In Thomas Loveless (Ed.), *The Great Curriculum Debate: How Should We Teach Reading and Math?* (pp. 42–84). Washington, DC: Brookings Press. (Based on a paper presented at the conference, "Curriculum Wars: Alternative Approaches to Reading and Mathematics." Harvard University, October 21–22, 1999.)

Battista, M. T. (2004). Applying Cognition-Based Assessment to Elementary School Students' Development of Understanding of Area and Volume Measurement. *Mathematical Thinking and Learning*, *6*(2): 185–204.

Battista, M. T., and Clements, D. H. (May 1996). Students' Understanding of Three-Dimensional Rectangular Arrays of Cubes. *Journal for Research in Mathematics Education*, *27*(3): 258–292.

Battista, M. T., Clements, D. H., Arnoff, J., Battista, K., and Borrow, C. V. A. (1998). Students' Spatial Structuring and Enumeration of 2D Arrays of Squares. *Journal for Research in Mathematics Education*, *29*(5): 503–532.

Black, P., and Wiliam, D. (1998). Raising Standards Through Classroom Assessment. *Phi Delta Kappan*, *80*(2): 139–148.

Bransford, J. D., Brown, A. L., and Cocking, R. R. (1999). *How People Learn: Brain, Mind, Experience, and School*. Washington, DC: National Research Council.

Buschman, L. (December 2001). Using Student Interviews to Guide Classroom Instruction: An Action Research Project. *Teaching Children Mathematics*, pp. 222–227.

Carpenter, T. P., and Fennema, E. (1991). Research and Cognitively Guided Instruction. In E. Fennema, T. P. Carpenter, and S. J. Lamon (Eds.), *Integrating Research on Teaching and Learning Mathematics* (pp. 1–16). Albany: State University of New York Press.

Carpenter, T. P., Franke, M. L., Jacobs, V. R., Fennema, E., and Empson, S. B. (1998). A Longitudinal Study of Invention and Understanding in Children's Multidigit Addition and Subtraction. *Journal for Research in Mathematics Education*, *29*(1): 3–20.

Cobb, P., and Wheatley, G. (1988). Children's Initial Understanding of Ten. *Focus on Learning Problems in Mathematics*, *10*(3): 1–28.

Cobb, P., Wood, T., Yackel, E., Nicholls, J., Wheatley, G., Trigatti, B., and Perlwitz, M. (1991). Assessment of a Problem-Centered Second-Grade Mathematics Project. *Journal for Research in Mathematics Education*, *22*(1): 3–29.

De Corte, E., Greer, B., and Verschaffel, L. (1996). Mathematics Teaching and Learning. In D. C. Berliner and R. C. Calfee (Eds.), *Handbook of Educational Psychology* (pp. 491–549). New York: Simon & Schuster Macmillan.

Fennema, E., Carpenter, T. P., Franke, M. L., Levi, L., Jacobs, V. R., and Empson, S. B. (1996). A Longitudinal Study of Learning to Use Children's Thinking in Mathematics Instruction. *Journal for Research in Mathematics Education*, *27*(4): 403–434.

Fennema, E., and Franke, M. L. (1992). Teachers' Knowledge and Its Impact. In D. A. Grouws (Ed.), *Handbook of Research on Mathematics Teaching* (pp. 127–164). Reston, VA: National Council of Teachers of Mathematics/Macmillan.

Fuson, K. C., Wearne, D., Hiebert, J. C., Murray, H. G., Human, P. G., Olivier, A. L., et al. (1997). Children's Conceptual Structures for Multidigit Numbers and Methods of Multidigit Addition and Subtraction. *Journal for Research in Mathematics Education*, *28*(2): 130–162.

Greeno, J. G., Collins, A. M., and Resnick, L. (1996). Cognition and Learning. In D. C. Berliner and R. C. Calfee (Eds.), *Handbook of Educational Psychology* (pp. 15–46). New York: Simon & Schuster Macmillan.

Hiebert, J., and Carpenter, T. P. (1992). Learning and Teaching with Understanding. In D. A. Grouws (Ed.), *Handbook of Research on Mathematics Teaching* (pp. 65–97). Reston, VA: National Council of Teachers of Mathematics/Macmillan.

Lester, F. K. (1994). Musing About Mathematical Problem-Solving Research: 1970–1994. *Journal for Research in Mathematics Education*, *25*(6): 660–675.

National Research Council. (1989). *Everybody Counts*. Washington, DC: National Academy Press, 1989.

Prawat, R. S. (1999). Dewey, Peirce, and the Learning Paradox. *American Educational Research Journal*, *36*(1): 47–76.

Romberg, T. A. (1992). Further Thoughts on the Standards: A Reaction to Apple. *Journal for Research in Mathematics Education*, *23*(5): 432–437.

Schoenfeld, A. C. (1994). What Do We Know About Mathematics Curricula. *Journal of Mathematical Behavior*, 13: 55–80.

Steffe, L. P. (1988). Children's Construction of Number Sequences and Multiplying Schemes. In J. Hiebert and M. Behr (Eds.), *Number Concepts and Operations in the Middle Grades* (pp. 119–140). Reston, VA: National Council of Teachers of Mathematics.

Steffe, L. P. (1992). Schemes of Action and Operation Involving Composite Units. *Learning and Individual Differences*, *4*(3): 259–309.

Steffe, L. P., and D'Ambrosio, B. S. (1995). Toward a Working Model of Constructivist Teaching: A Reaction to Simon. *Journal for Research in Mathematics Education*, *26*(2): 146–159.

Steffe, L. P., and Kieren, T. (1994). Radical Constructivism and Mathematics Education. *Journal for Research in Mathematics Education*, *25*(6): 711–733.

van Hiele, P. M. (1986). *Structure and Insight*. Orlando, FL: Academic Press.

von Glasersfeld, E. (1995). *Radical Constructivism: A Way of Knowing and Learning*. Washington, DC: Falmer Press.